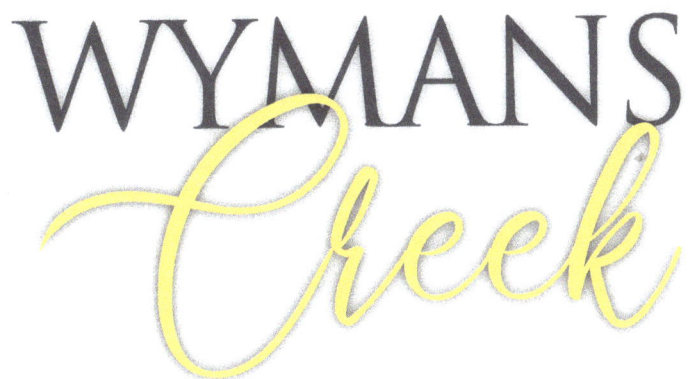

WYMANS Creek

MARGARET (MARJORI) WIESE

PRIMIX
PUBLISHING
THE WRITE CHOICE

Primix Publishing
East Brunswick Office Evolution
1 Tower Center Boulevard, Ste 1510
East Brunswick, NJ 08816
www.primixpublishing.com
Phone: 1-800-538-5788

All photos are taken by Albertine (Tena)Ellinwood. Except personal photos of Margaret Wiese and Margene Wiese-Baier

The photo's also include free ones from the Internet.

To contact Margene Wiese-Baier at designsbysunwhisp8@gmail.com
Also, on Facebook... Margene Wiese-Baier
Also known as Sunwhisp

ISBN: 979-8-89194-197-7(sc)
ISBN: 979-8-89194-198-4(e)

Library of Congress Control Number: 2024911252

Published by Primix Publishing: 12/11/2024

$\mathcal{Contents}$

Dedication

Mom and Dad's photo.

Margaret Ann Wicklund-Wiese, left her four children and her husband a Legacy of her Novels among other treasures wrapped up in her Writing. Throughout her lifetime, our memory of our Mother consisted of her sitting almost daily at her typewriter and her fingers tapping on the keys as fast as she could type. The words just seemed to flow to her fingertips. She would stop to visit with anyone that would stop by to visit. She seemed to always have time for her family and friends. She was loved by many.

Mom gave us girls jobs around the house to make sure the house stayed tidy, and the boys chopped firewood and brought it in to keep the fire burning. And they had chores of their own. Sometimes, Mom even hired a friend to clean the house, so she could keep writing. Each of us can remember the times that we sat on the end of her bed while she read to us from her writings. Some were children's stories, and some were more grown up. Mom would make it so interesting we were sometimes late for School. It was always worth it because we had that time with her. She created in all of us a Love for Writing. She shared with us her Passion. She had a flare for writing Novels, Short Stories, Poetry, but she also had a love for Music. She loved the Country and Western Music that always had a story to tell. She had help writing the music that went along with her Songs. Even though she did not have the best singing voice, she would sing her songs into a recorder that she could type as she listened to it over and over again. Mom was multitalented and also did the Artwork for her Indian books.

My dad to this day tells of sneaking in to read some of her writ- ing and told me that someone wanted to make a Movie out of one of her Stories, but she wanted to get it Published into a book first. My Dad was always proud of her and encouraged her to go to the different places to see if she could get her books published. Without my Dad and his encouragement for me to keep moving forward, my Mom's writing to get published might stay a Dream and not become a Reality. I will always be grateful that even when I did not have faith in myself to get things done, he stood beside me and told me that I could do it. Sometimes in one's own lifetime, Dreams are not accomplished but passed on for someone in the family to fulfill. Dad has been my Partner in getting these books done. Mom had a way of making each one of us feel special and could inspire us all to use our gifts and talents! I was Artistic, so she encouraged me to do Artwork and also write. My oldest brother Curt wrote also. My brother Dan followed in my Dad's footsteps and took on the trade of Saw Filer. He worked alongside my Dad, sharpening the big Saws for the Saw Mills. My Brother Curt also followed in my

Dad's footsteps for a time and then moved to areas where he could be closer to Nature and was able to use the Animals for the bases of his stories. Later being called Mountain Man and an Old Cowboy because he Looked like some of the Movie Cowboys in his later years and even wrote Western Novels.

My Sister Tami is a writer also and has Published many of her own books and has memories of going to the Post Office and mailing Mom's Novels to different Publishers. The Postman would always ask her how much she wanted to insure the packages for and my sister would say a Million dollars. To all of us, Mom's books and the Legacy she left is worth oh so much more.

My Mom was the best Mom any son or daughter could have. She was born November 17, 1925, to Parents Gustaf A. Wicklund and Alvina Wicklund (born Eiffler). Mom grew up on a small farm in Minnesota with her brothers and sisters. She had a love for reading books from a young age. She would also go out and sit on the fence gate and imagine what her life would be and would also yodel. She had a great Love for Jesus that she passed on to her children. My Dad and her brought all her children up going to a Lutheran Church like her Parents did with her and her siblings. She taught us to call on Jesus when we had nightmares and pray the Lord's Prayer and say the Twenty-Third Psalm and a little Prayer that she wrote that also blessed the whole family including Grandparents and Aunts and Uncles Cousins etc. (Now I lay me down to sleep, Angels guard my little Nest! Glad and well may I wake! I ask it all for Jesus sake! Amen and Amen! God bless Mommy, Daddy, Curtis Jr., Daniel, Tami, and, and, and!) Mom taught us the Golden rule. Mainly what I remember is that she rarely said anything about anyone unless it was something good. My Mom was not perfect, but she tried to be loving to all. She followed Jesus all throughout her life and went to Heaven June of 1985. I am thankful she taught me about Jesus from a young age, and that lets me know that someday, I will see her again in Heaven.

No matter what she was told by the Publishers, she persevered and kept Writing, my brother Curt told me. She knew that God gave her a great gift, and she was going to use it. I know she is still writing in

Heaven. She came to me in a dream and asked me to get her books published. I argued with her in the dream that I did not know how, but she won out in the dream, and I am going to do my best to get her books and other writing published. Without my family and friend's encouragement, more time would go by and the books would not get done. So with getting her works Published, her Legacy will be carried on. Not only to be Treasured by her family, but for all those that read them.

I know that she tried throughout her lifetime and she searched for the right Publisher. Many Loved her work, and some told her that her writing was before its time, so all these years later, it is time to Make her Dreams come true and to make her Legacy of Love a Reality.

Love, Margene

Introduction

Wymans Creek is just one of Mom's novels but is where I felt led to start. A story of a Family on the Journey of Life that not only tells of their family, but the people that they were involved with. The people that without them there would be no story. This story will grip your heart in knowing that no matter what happens in life…Life goes on. Rachel, the main character, is courageous throughout the story. She has been thrown some things throughout her life that most people could not have endured. This story shows that Women have strength and can endure if put to the test. Lister, Rachel's Aunt, is the cornerstone of the family that reads her Bible and prays over the family and loves Jesus with all of her Heart! Wilkins, the main male character, is thrown a challenge in this story that will show that he is a better man than he realizes. There are twists and turns in this story of this family that shows what people go through in this Journey we call Life. I hope you enjoy reading this story. It is full of Action and Suspense, but also is a lesson of what we can all endure if faced with the challenges of Life.

—Margene Wiese-Baier

Chapter 1

RACHEL'S HOMECOMING

In 1922, after spending two years in San Francisco studying art, Rachel Lansing came back to Wymans Creek.

The train slowly clanged down the grade. Rachel clasped her hands together, feeling a sense of suspended elation at the famil- iar sights. The Northside of town lay like a peach pit sunk into the flesh of the fruit, its soggy marsh land cratering rundown company houses. The heat of the August sun beat against the window, but she could see sandbags still piled along the creek as a reminder of ram- pant spring runoffs, when the snow melted in the mountains and ravaged the lowlands.

The sawmill, tin-sided and monstrous, zigzagged to fit the pattern of the creek, ballooned to hold logs, corralled like floating steers fattened for slaughter. Shooting flames spit through the door of the wigwam burner, as it caught the waste and hurled blue-streaked smoke into the air obstructing the sight of the mountains. Even inside the train, Rachel could hear the shrill gratifying whine of the mill machinery. It was a sound that was absent when she left. The mill was shut down, the quietness was disturbing, and it meant hard- ship for the people.

The train screeched to a sudden halt at the depot door. Rachel grasped a small worn satchel and walked to the end of the loading dock where a team of matched mares stood lazily switching their tails as the cargo of sacked grain was unloaded. Swinging the sacks to the lumbering cart was a woman in her early fifties. Cloaked in a gigantic knit shawl, she reminded Rachel of a monk.

Two years hadn't changed Aunt Lister. Rachel noted the graying hair pulled severely off the furrowed brow.

The older woman roughly brushed her hand across her eyes at the sight of her niece.

"It's good to have you home again," she said, taking the valise from Rachel and tossing it into the rear of the wagon. She helped Rachel to the wagon seat, then climbed up un-ladylike and sat beside her, clutching to the reins with one hand, bringing the whip cracking into the air with the other.

"It's nice to be back," Rachel mumbled, regaining her compo- sure after the abrupt departure. Lister Wyman glanced occasionally at the passenger beside her but spoke very little, concentrating on guiding the team through the town.

No other sounds reached Rachel's ears, save for the monoto- nous rhythm of the lone wagon's droning wheels and the continuous clickety-clack of horse's feet and jangling harness chains.

Fresh scents infiltrated the air. Green hay, ripening grain, the pungent odor of decaying fruits and the pitchy flames of the mill.

In the two years in which she was in San Francisco, Wymans Creek hadn't grown. It had diminished into an oasis devoid of progress. Only occasionally did she see an automobile or anything to remind her of the city. Pony posts and plank walks without a trace of life. The church doors opened to the public, empty inside. A pale glow shone in the window of Dr. Stein's cottage.

Jake's Hardware and Wymans Creek Grocery had the shades drawn in strict adherence to an open at six, close at five policy.

Men stood near the swinging doors of the saloon, cursing and laughing. That hadn't changed. Aunt Lister had often referred to the tavern as Satan's den; now they passed the establishment without remarks.

"I certainly hope you didn't adopt the rough and crude ways of your Bohemian associates." Lister suddenly brought the team to a halt and turned on the gravel creek road.

"What makes you say that, Aunt Lister?"

"I'm not blind—you've raised your skirts, rouged your lips. And what have you done to your hair? Looked better in pigtails."

"After all, I'm going to be twenty, that's a little old for pigtails.

Don't you think I've changed for the better?"

"I hope so! Not that I have the right to say it, but I see more of your mother in you now than ever. Mind you, I didn't say you'd do the things she does, but you do have her good looks. Sometimes, beauty isn't a blessing."

"Oh, Auntie, I don't mind it anymore when you say I'm like her. She loves music the way I love the canvas. Everything else has to take second place. Anyway, I didn't see Mama. She was on tour. Was that how you planned it? I could live in her flat while I took art lessons. She'd be thousands of miles away and I couldn't see her. Will I ever see her again?"

"Heaven forbid!" Lister pulled at her glove, then cracked the whip, startling the team with sadistic gusto.

"I hear you have one of your paintings in the gallery already," Lister said.

Rachel's reply was lost in the sound of crunching gravel as the team turned down the narrow lane. They passed the Old Indian Woman's shack; tar-papered and dilapidated, it seemed to grow into the hillside. In the shadows, Rachel could see the old woman on her knees along the creek bed, gathering herbs.

Lister held the team to a slower pace. Branches from the overhanging trees brushed the horses' backs. A butterfly skimmed, touching the ear of one of the horses, then swiftly flitted over and around the team to alight ahead of them on a clump of dusty queen's lace.

Climbing jaggedly uphill, the road followed the creek. Green scum floated on the water. Rachel sighed. Dog days, she couldn't swim in the hottest part of August.

It was not yet night, but a pale star looked white in the still blue sky. A willow branch brushed Rachel's cheek, then heavy board planks creaked as the wagon groaned over the loosened boards of the narrow bridge. The three miles from town to the ranch had seemed like twenty miles of churning and grinding on the wagon seat.

As Rachel stepped from the wagon, blue jays swept down toward her in anger, scolding, reminding her that she was a stranger to them.

She was home. Home. The big white house sheltered by spindly trees and mapped with flower gardens everywhere. Red and yellow roses blooming until frost nipped their last buds. A wild grape vine rambled up the lattice of the back porch, climbing to reach the window of the balcony.

To Rachel, it seemed the foliage had grown around the house; until now, the house looked small—like a child's drawing. A square box. Peaked roof, smoke curling from a stone chimney. Windows: millions of tiny glass panes. The window to Rachel's room was open. A draft had sucked the curtain to the outside, holding it while it flapped.

Lister tied the team to the hitching post and went inside. Rachel stayed behind, drinking in the freshness and newness of the country air. How beautiful everything seemed! But all the beauty of the universe could not conceal her memory of her two years in San Francisco. Her two years with Paul.

It was like being lost. A child stumbling through a forest. Now, half of her was found. The other half still at large. A million miles apart. It was both joy and agony to remember, but she always would! Nothing could change that—even Aunt Lister was aware of it. In two years, she had become woman. A complete woman, whose arms, lips, and soul ached because a name refused to leave her mind. Rachel pressed her fingers tightly against her eyes, forcefully trying to dim the sight of him.

"Rachel," Lister's voice penetrated the blankness.

"I'm on the veranda," Rachel answered flippantly. "It's so good to feel the fresh air. I had almost forgotten what it's like."

"You'd better come in. Wilkins is beginning to think you have bees in your bonnet."

Wilkins! Lister Wyman's stepson. For the first time in months, Rachel thought of him. Wilkins and the summer house. She trembled. Funny, she thought, the mere repeating of a name can rekindle emotions, both pleasant and repugnant in one instance.

She took a deep breath. "I'll be right in—in just a moment." There was no mistaking the scent of tobacco and shaving lotion.

Wilkins touched her arm, pressing his fingers into her flesh. "You're sure looking good, Rachel."

"It's...it's nice to be back."

His hand lingered on her arm. Teasingly, she removed it. Consciously conveying a message, a promise. Wilkins watched her tap lightly on the library door.

"Come in." Lister removed the sewing from the chair next to the work table. "Milk or tea? You look worn."

"Tea, please. I'm not really tired. I was so anxious to get home, now I almost feel as if I shouldn't have come."

"Nonsense," Lister said, continuing with her sewing.

Rachel held the cup to her lips. Knowing it was expected of her, she asked, "Has Wilkins been in good health?"

"Wilkins is well." Lister looked into Rachel's eyes. "He misses Mary some. Another wife would be the best thing in the world for him."

"Another wife?" she asked shocked. "Mary's only been gone a year. Has it been a year?"

"Year come February. Men are different than women. Your Uncle

Rex, bless his soul, has been gone fifteen years. I haven't had the need for another man."

Rachel looked at the straight body ungraced by femininity. It was hard to believe her aunt had ever been caressed by a man. Lister was only nineteen when she married Rex Wyman, a man over thirty years her senior. Rachel sighed. Lister was never young and pretty. Rachel could remember her own mother, and she was both young and beautiful.

Mama was touring with a road show when she brought Rachel to the big ranch to live with Aunt Lister. Rachel was only five then. Sometimes, she would dream about her mother, and when she awoke, she was crying. Sometimes, she cried all night long.

Noting the faraway look in Rachel's face, Lister jolted her back to reality. "Wilkins is still young. He needs a family. My happiest days were when you both were children. Couldn't have a child of my own, but I raised you both like my own." She paused, seeking to catch Rachel's reaction. "Wilkins is a fine specimen of a man. I think he's glad you're home."

Rachel felt an excitement. *True,* she thought, *he's a fine speci- men— all six feet of him. The dark curly hair, those smoldering eyes.*

The room was soundless except for the soft rustling of mate- rial as Lister folded and unfolded the yards of multicolored fabric, blinding Rachel until she felt scrambled on the inside.

"Auntie," she said. "I'm going up to bed. I didn't realize I was so worn."

The curtain was still billowing outside. She drew it in and closed the window. Her room was aired, and the bed freshly made, blankets turned back. Aunt Lister always made her bed like that. It had been a hard and tiring trip, and she crept between the cold ironed sheets.

"Oh!" she wept. "Will I ever be in his arms again?"

Darkness covered her, but she felt alive—alive in her memories of San Francisco.

What an empty feeling it was to be alone in a city so immense that the comprehension of it was nearly impossible. Her feet were swollen from the long tedious train ride. She sat for a long time on a hard bench by the window. A man handed her a note. Her mother was on tour, and the apartment was only eight blocks from the depot. Street cars clanged back and forth on the streets, but she walked.

Eight blocks that seemed like eight miles.

Climbing up hills and almost falling down them. Ragged apartment houses jutted haphazardly along winding, narrow streets. The suitcase weighed her down, then she was knocking on a door that had a tin plate, Manager.

The landlady sized Rachel up, shook her head, and led her to a door with a big metal seven tacked on it. She unlocked the door. "If you need anything just holler. Your ma and me have sort of a pact. I don't care how she lives, and she don't bother me none."

Baggy eyed and crinkly haired, the old woman made Rachel's flesh crawl.

"You sure look like your ma, dearie."

The door closed behind her. Tears flooded Rachel's eyes and she shook. Aunt Lister was right. Her mother was a loose woman, even the landlady hinted that. What an awful world.

Collapsing on the bed, she let her shoes fall to the floor. Tears slid down her cheeks onto the satin bed covering, and she lay and counted the cracks in the ceiling until her eyes could no longer focus.

It was blustery and dismal when she awakened. Low-hanging fog engulfed the city like an omen. After her nap, she was hungry and turned the gas light up, searching the cupboards for food. To the right of the living room was a kitchen and there was a bath. It had a real bathtub, not a laundry tub, and water came from a faucet. Some velvety hand towels hung on a rack and she took one, holding it against her face.

The towels smelled clean. Mama can't be all bad. She remem- bered the scent of her mother's dressing room. Fresh cut flowers. Forgetting her hunger, she sat back down on the bed, her fingers gliding over the smooth bed covering.

"Mama," she whispered. "Why didn't you take me with you?"

Noisy street cars and people bustling by on the street outside the window were the only reply to her painful question. Everything was so different from Wymans Creek. The sawmill made noise, but she was used to that. Thinking about the meeting with the landlady, she felt a sudden tolerance for the world outside. There are all kinds of people. Some are happy. Some are sad. She felt sandwiched some- where between, neither happy nor sad.

Aunt Lister had given her money for her art lessons. Counting out the bills one by one, she divided the money neatly into two piles. There was some clothing in the bureau drawer, and she hid some of the money under the clothes. She pinned the rest to her chemise.

Memories stumbled around in her mind as she ran the water high in the bathtub. The water was nearly cold when she stepped out of it. Aunt Lister had packed her long flannel nightgown with faded yellow roses. She hated it! Rolling the gown into a tight ball, she put it back into her suitcase. The sheets felt slippery against her body and she shivered.

Tomorrow, she thought, "I'll start my lessons from Paul Nielson. Even his name seemed disconnected from art." Then she was slipping off again, into a slumbering world while foreign ringing names of bygone artists tumbled through her mind.

Chapter 2

PAUL NIELSON, THE ART TEACHER

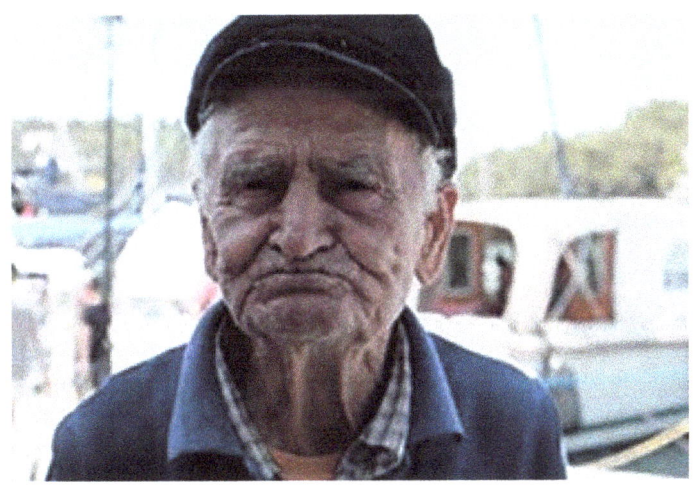

Paul Nielson glanced up from his easel, shocked to see the girl standing there.

"What do you want?" He did not react deliberately, embarrassed at the cool appraisal. "Wasn't expecting anyone," he grumbled.

Rachel fumbled with her gloves. "I'm Rachel Lansing. My Aunt, Lister Wyman, wrote you. I'm to study under you."

A soiled piece of cloth fell to the floor. Paul grappled for it to dab up some paint that seemed to fly from his brush. This girl had a strange effect on him; he had anticipated someone older. He placed the brush in a jar of turpentine.

"I didn't expect you until the fifteenth." "It is the fifteenth," Rachel gulped.

"Well, I'll be! Get my days a bit messed up sometimes."

Picking out another brush, he continued to paint as if Rachel was not in the room.

Rachel retired receptively to a chair. How dare he treat her in such a rude manner? So this is the Bohemian Personality Aunt Lister spoke of. Artists and writers. She wondered why talent had to be labeled.

On the train, she had formed a mental image of what Paul Nielson looked like. Expecting to see a bearded Van Gogh, but Paul was not an old man. He wasn't a very big man either, but she could tell he was strong because of his arms. Blond hairs grew thick on his arms and high on his chest. His shirt was unbuttoned, and the sleeves were rolled up above the elbow. Wilkins kept his shirt buttoned all the way down and wore his cuffs tight. She swallowed recalling how tight Wilkins's collar looked when his Adam's apple moved up and down.

A realistic landscape, with blue-green ocean waves and a sunset emerged on the canvas, but Rachel saw only the artist. Mentally, she stroked her finger down the line of his nose.

It was slightly off center. She felt the expanse of his forehead, noticing he held his lips taut as he worked. His chin, she surmised, is determined—a cleft in the center is a sure sign of self-centeredness.

Their eyes met. Paul strolled to the window and opened it. He was perspiring and appeared to work under intense pressure.

"Well, that's it for now." He stood back from the painting as if not quite pleased with it. "Sorry you had to wait, but that's how it goes."

"I didn't mind. I liked watching you. Your picture, it's lovely, it's as if I were there—feeling the spray on my face!"

Paul set the palette aside and cleaned the brushes. When he finished with the brushes, he sorted them and put them in jars with the bristles sticking up. Without looking at Rachel, he unrolled his shirt sleeves and put a tweedy-looking coat on. He still looked unkempt.

"I'd give anything to paint like that!" she said.

The artist studied the girl. "It takes talent and guts to make it as an artist. Very few get rich, but if you've got something on the ball you eat."

"Oh, Aunt Lister thinks I have talent. Art and music run in our family."

"Who is Aunt Lister?"

Tears burned Rachel's eyes. "She's my aunt. She studied art in Paris. Would have made it too—only she married my Uncle Rex. There was too much to do on the ranch. She didn't have time to paint."

"I could use some grub," he said, admiring the fortitude of the girl who held her eyes to his as he spoke. "Get hungrier as a bear when I'm working. There's a place down the street."

The coffee shop right down the street turned out to be several blocks from the studio. Rachel found it a chore keeping pace with his long strides. When they arrived, he sat down at the counter. She crowded in next to him.

"Hungry?" he asked.

"No," she said truthfully. "I just want coffee."

The aroma of food reminded her that she was famished, but her stomach was doing the flip-flops.

Sipping daintily from her cup, Rachel watched annoyed as Paul ate with relish but without manners.

"How old are you?" he asked. "Eighteen," she said, wanting to lie.

"Eighteen, eighteen is just a runny nosed brat." "I could lie—say I'm twenty?"

"Cripes, kid, I've been around." Anger shone in Rachel's eyes.

"No offense!" he said, raising his hands as if he needed protec- tion from her possible physical retaliation.

Her coffee cup empty, she watched in amazement as he blew cigarette smoke in perfect circles over her.

"Ever been in Frisco before?" he asked.

"I was born here," she said positively, "but I've lived in Wymans Creek since I was five. Ever hear of Wymans Creek? We live on a ranch, hundreds of acres."

"That figures, fresh but old-fashioned. That get-up you're wear- ing went out of style seasons ago."

Rachel jumped to her feet. "I'm sorry, Mr. Nielson. I'm sorry you don't approve of what I'm wearing. I like it!" She started for the door, then returned to the table, dropping a dime in front of him. "For the coffee."

Her outburst amused him. "See you tomorrow, Ms. Lansing. Eight-thirty sharp. And if you don't mind my suggestion, wear some- thing more comfortable. You'll be on your feet for a long time."

"I hate him! I hate him already." She fretted starting the long walk back to her flat.

She walked briskly with angry steps. The ladies she met on the streets were elegantly dressed in chic white blouses and skirts of blue, lavender, or pink. She was despaired at her own dress, outdated and mousy gray. Old-fashioned!

Rachel clasped her hand to the inside of her blouse, feeling for the outline of the safety pin that held her money safe. Still there. The manikin in the window was dressed in scarlet.

Like a hussy, she mused. The dress had a fitted bodice and flow- ing skirt.

"I want to buy the dress in the window," she announced to the gaping clerk.

"Your size, miss?"

"It will fit, I know it will. And I want to try on some shoes— some comfortable walking shoes," she added, first catching her breath.

The clerk wrapped the dress in tissue paper while Rachel poked her feet into various styles of shoes. Finding the ones she wanted, she walked around in circles in front of the mirror.

"I really like these."

"Will that be all, ma'am?" the clerk said, impatient for her to remove the shoes.

"I'll wear them—if you don't mind." Awkwardly, she reached for the money in its hiding place. The clerk watched annoyed. Her old shoes lay on the carpet at his feet.

"Your shoes?"

Rachel was already out the door.

It had been a grueling day, and the walk to the apartment was farther than she had expected. Her feet were red and swollen when she took the new shoes off. She left them off for a while, then she put them back on. By tomorrow, she would be used to them, even if she had to wear them all night.

The dress fit, and she pretended she was a glamorous model, gliding around in different poses. Brushing her hair, she dug the bristles into her scalp until it hurt. Gathering her hair into a ball, securing it with the string from the package the dress came in. She wet her fingertips and formed tiny ringlets framing her forehead and temples. She dabbed lip rouge from the container on her mother's dresser, across her lips. Never again would a man tell her she was unstylish, especially Paul, that uncouth contemptible man! After primping, she was hungry. There was a can of meat and she opened it and sliced a thick piece of it, putting it between two slices of stale bread, like a Bohemian. The evening passed quickly.

Moments of the day screened before her eyes. *Someday, I'll be a great artist,* she promised. *Someday, I'll show Paul.*

Promptly, at eight-thirty the next morning, Rachel was at the studio. Paul's eyes glowed in appreciation at the metamorphosis. Rachel glared back at him defiantly. He was wearing a wrinkled robe and had not shaved. She felt as if she had entered his bedroom.

"I'm sorry if I'm early, but you said eight-thirty." "That's what I said. Know how to stretch a canvas?" "Yes, Aunt Lister—"

"Set up," he interrupted. "I'll be with you in a jiffy and dump those shoes before you break your neck."

How she hated him and how her feet hurt. Blisters were killing her.

Minutes later, he returned clean shaven, his chin patched with small bits of newsprint.

"Planning on limping around all day?"

She didn't answer him, fumbling as she tacked down the canvas. Before she realized what was happening, he drew her to a chair and groped at her feet, trying to remove her shoes.

"You have pretty legs," he said, his voice raspy. He paused, thinking about his abrupt actions, then patted her knee. "Wasn't what I had in mind for the first lesson, but I do think I have a willing student."

She wanted to scream at him. She wasn't cheap or a tramp that he could insult. But something she didn't quite understand happened to her and she looked at him with a new yearning inside. "Is there somewhere I can make some coffee?" she asked, acting very calm.

"The pot's right in there." He pointed to a small room with a skinny closet-like door. "I'll take mine black—one spoon of sugar."

That first day, she had learned a lesson. Paul Nielson was the instructor. She was his student. There would never be a touch nor a glance to betray her. Working beside him, letting his hand guide her brush stroke. The choking sensation of closeness she wanted to share with him but refused to show it. A lingering hand on her arm, soft breaths caressing her neck. The tenseness of wanting, but not receiving—stifled by her own sheer willpower and self-deception.

Frightened and angry at feelings that seemed to ebb and flow, from joy to sadness to ardent desires to cold appraisal. Days into months—months that stamped the basic fundamentals of art securely in her mind.

Techniques, mediums, textures, balance, and perspective had been ground into her brain until she cried out for expression. She knew she could paint, if only she could glimpse the scene her mind could record, then transpose it on canvas. Experimenting in colors: vibrant or solemn hues, with various degrees of shadings. Doubts seeped in. What if she couldn't paint what she felt? What if she could only sketch the things her eyes saw, failing to capture the true values she felt as she dabbled with colors?

And she painted. Splashes of forms and colors. San Francisco's elaborate architectural buildings, assorted cereal boxes with cut-out windows. Portraits with blank faces, expressionless eyes and mouth.

Like the dead fish she had seen lying on the beach after a storm. Blank eyes, dead eyes, empty faces with no eyes at all.

Paul laughed at her fears, reassuring her that talent needed development.

Did she have that talent? She wept, fearful she could never paint as well as he could.

She had spent nearly two years setting her easel beside Paul's, watching while his deft hand painted with professionalism, feeling that hers lacked his approach.

Today, they felt the tranquility of the rushing, constant sea. Two-minute specks large only in comparison to the blue jellyfish that had washed ashore. The beach stretched for miles and miles—etched by bruised seaweed and bleached driftwood.

Rachel followed closely after Paul, carrying her easel and paint box. The sun was warm, and childishly, they stopped to play, build- ing castles in the sand. Drawing pictures with a slim piece of drift- wood. Writing their names in large childish scrawls, chasing each other wildly back and forth, running in the water.

Exhausted, they dropped to rest. Paul restless and eager. Rachel weary from the long walk and rough play.

"Want to play a perceptive game?" Paul asked. "I'm tired, I want to rest first."

"This won't make you tired—it's to make you more aware of your senses. Close your eyes."

Rachel closed her eyes. "I can't see anything."

"Yes, you can see. Your memory records all the images you have seen. Sights, smells, sounds, tastes, touch. All of the senses are work- ing even when your eyes are closed."

She closed her eyes and lay very still. "Yeah, I know what you mean. I smell salty water. Not really—ugh. Fishy. I feel a spray across my face." She licked her lips. "I taste the salt."

"What do you hear? Keep your eyes closed," he said, moving closer to her.

"Seagulls screaming. I hear a dog barking—not barking, sort of yipping. Must be a little dog. Some men are talking, but their voices are a long way off. Paul," she sat up quickly. "I can hear your heart beating."

"Keep your eyes closed," he said, his body touching hers. "Put out your hand," he said, dropping some sand in her hand.

"Do you know what that is?" "Sand—it's warm and grainy."

He touched her face. She held her hand over his, feeling the hairy roughness.

"Your hand is warm," she said, holding it to her lips. He kissed her mouth, first gently then urgently.

"You tricked me!" she said, springing up quickly, looking at him with both pleasure and surprise. "I thought we were going to paint." "I didn't intend to do that," he said getting to his feet. "It's late, we'd better get back."

"I'll come later," she called to him as he started to stroll down the beach. "I'm going to paint my masterpiece."

The tide was coming in before she got to her feet to leave. Gulls gathered, and she watched as they swept into the wild surf, balancing delicately on the crest of the waves.

Fishermen secured their boats and stood around the docks talking about their day's catch. As she walked down the board planks, the men followed her with their eyes. She wanted to run.

Clutching the easel under her arm, fingers holding tightly to the paints, she searched for the subject. The seascape—red and coral horizon. Boats of every description—cabin, dories, commercial, pleasure craft. Boats of every color secured by knotted ropes. Rising and falling with the surges of the tide.

Fog drifted in, obscuring the horizon. Dusk was saturated with a dampening mist that glazed the fishermen's black rubberized cloth- ing, making them look like skating penguins.

Rachel walked past a lonely figure almost unseen in the fog. A dog nipped at her heels, frightening her. She cringed. A voice called to the dog, and a blurred outline closed in on her. A lined, weary face with sunken eyes. White hair straining from beneath a tightly knit stocking cap, an old man with heavy shoes, a bent back and knotty hands.

"They'll be coming in any time now," the old man said as if he were talking to someone he knew.

Rachel studied him. The perfect face for a portrait.

A rustic background, yards of nets, weather-beaten boats.

Eyes—she had seen his eyes. Looking into them, she felt the torture he was feeling—sharing his doom. In a fleeting moment, she had captured him in her mind.

"She's like a woman," he said, his eyes still cast to-ward the sea.

"You get to love her, and you try to hold her close to you. But you get old, and she opens her arms to the young ones.

You don't forget her though. She's got a hold on you and you just watch her, knowing she ain't got use for someone who can't sat- isfy her. My eyes are bad—don't have the strength in my hands any- more. Can't handle the gear.

"My sons, they fish—pretty soon my grandsons. But I love her. She gets in your blood. Don't have much time left, but I want to live my last days watching her. Knowing I've courted her with the best of them. I...I...I..."

A warning whistle of a small boat interrupted the old man's speech. Without looking back at Rachel, he walked slowly down the docks.

Riding the streetcar back to the city, Rachel could feel the sea, smell the sea. She held in her mind the picture of the old fisherman, and she knew now that she could paint.

Lined and weary, the old man's face was always in her mind. She saw every crevice, knew how his nostrils flared only slightly. But she could not paint him. The colors in his face wasn't blended right. Depths and contours of his jaw failed to please her. There were only empty sockets for eyes. She tried again. Daily searching for the old man, but he was gone, and she could only paint from memory. In desperation, she kept trying. She had worked too hard on it, so now, she painted only a few hours a day. Wild brush strokes angered her, and she demanded perfection.

Another week passed, then something seemed to press in on her, urging the portrait to completion. When it was finished, it was Paul who exclaimed with pride, "Rachel, you're a pro—you have to show this one."

Show it? She had painted the old man because she had to. The painting had become some inner part of her and she didn't want to share it.

It was as if the model and the artist shared some deep secret. That secret was not to be exposed to a world of gaping art seekers.

"What if it doesn't sell? What if no one wants it?" Rachel questioned, feeling a frightening agony—the fear that someone may take the painting from her or the fear it wasn't good enough.

"It'll sell. It's got it! Right down to the look of despair in the old man's eyes," Paul said, confident that he had coached an artist of great potential. "We'll celebrate. My first student to receive recogni- tion among the great."

He joyfully swung her around to face him. "You name it, Rachel, dinner, dancing, the works."

The next day, Rachel didn't go to the studio. She slept until midafternoon, then she got up and made some coffee and toast. When she finished eating, she went back to bed, dozing throughout the rest of the day. There was an emptiness inside her—at the same time a knowledge that she had accomplished something that left her with relief.

Low-hanging fog was clinging to the walk when she awakened. She watched Paul as he walked toward her apartment but deliberately hesitated in answering his persistent rapping. Something nagged her. She had worked closely beside him; in all that time, she had stub- bornly concealed her true feelings.

Intimate overtures had been made, but she sidetracked the issue. "Paul," she had said. "I'm going to be an artist. I can't share that love with anyone."

"You were willing to give yourself to me once. What happened to that girl?"

"That girl was me a hundred years ago," then she blurted. "Do you know what a woman feels when she loves a man and is left won- dering if he loves her—like something cheap?"

He did not answer her.

Later, they sat in a restaurant where small tables were tucked in and out of small alcoves. Impressed with the candlelit atmosphere, Rachel, eager and childlike, thumbed through the pages of the menu trying to make out the print in the dimness.

"I want fried chicken. Aunt Lister used to make it every Friday for supper."

Paul motioned to the waiter. A moodiness swept over Rachel and she sat staring into space.

Paul, anxious to please her, asked. "Anything else you'd like to do tonight? It's your night."

"You'd think I was crazy if I told you."

"Tell me. A crazy night deserves crazy desires," he said, reaching for her hand.

"It's silly, but I warned you. I want to go for a long walk. That's first. Then I want to dangle my feet in cold, cold water—just like I used to in Wymans Creek. And, Paul, I just want to be happy. I want you to be happy."

Paul felt her excitement. "I've got it! I know just the place. It's a little park—not many people go there. There is a lot of water and the pigeons and ducks so you'll have to watch where you're sitting, on the benches."

"Paul, I want to go home." "We've just got here."

"I don't mean my flat. I want to go home to Wymans Creek." "Rachel, you're homesick. You'll get over it."

"No, I won't, not till I go home again." "What about the artist?"

"That doesn't seem important anymore."

"For Pete's sake," Paul said fearfully. "Rachel, you've opened the door, you got a foot in it. How many artists spend a lifetime trying to get in? They never make it."

"I know that! I've just got to go back—I don't know why. I just do."

Evening slipped away into an obscure darkness. Paul took his shirt off, tossing it carelessly to a bench.

Paul turned away from her.

"Look at me, Paul. Why do you always make me feel so shameful? You paint your models. Why do you make me feel so wicked?" He didn't answer!

The park was everything Paul promised. Rachel raced ahead of him, frolicking, taking the pins from her hair, letting the wind whip through it.

A shallow stream rippled through cool green grasses, weaving a pathway through the park. She tore her shoes and hose from her feet and ran through the water laughing and playing, splashing cool water onto Paul as her pleasure excited him. Suddenly, a sadness crept over her and she stepped from the water, urging Paul to sit beside her.

"I'm happy," she whispered doubtfully.

Holding her close, he kissed her. "You're so beautiful," he whispered, stroking her damp hair back from her face.

"I don't feel beautiful," she said, drawing away from him. "Paul, it's just like home—the green grass, the birds, the quietness. Only it isn't home. It's different."

"It is different. You're not home."

"Paul, I can't ever feel like I did when I was a little girl—not ever again."

"I believe you. I wouldn't want you to be a little girl again." "You don't know what I mean," she said, impatient with him. "I don't either—only I feel like I've lost something. Something I can't ever find again."

Crickets chirped, and something frightened some ducks that took to the air quacking loudly. Rachel crept closer to him.

Rachel kissed him.

"You blocked my every move until now."

"You never told me you loved me. You can't say 'I love you.' A woman needs to be told she's loved—even if it isn't true."

"I love you, I do," Paul said to her.

Rachel sat up quickly as if trying to protect her virtue "When I was little, I tried to do everything Aunt Lister told me to do, just so she'd come to my room before I went to sleep. She'd tell me I was a good girl, not like my mama."

A faraway look came to her eyes. "All my life I've heard that Mama was no good. She was no good because she wasn't married when I was born."

Paul held her to him. "What your mother is or did has nothing to do with you. I love you. I love you, Rachel, but I can't marry you. I can't offer you that."

Rachel sat up abruptly. "I want to know about her—your wife." It would be the same lie his models smirked about. She also knew that she would believe anything he said, wishing she could hurt him for betraying her.

"She's in an institution. She doesn't know me, but I'm married to her. I always will be. I see her once a month, and I can't tell you what

I go through. She sits in this corner, holding a piece of cloth like it was the baby we lost." Agony of the words shown in his eyes.

"Forgive me," Rachel said tormented. "I didn't have the right to ask about her. I thought you were using excuses, so you wouldn't have to get involved."

"I'm not a saint. I never intended to give anyone that impres- sion. I didn't try to hide my marriage—from you or anyone else."

"No, Paul, you didn't. It doesn't seem fair."

"You're such a kid," he said holding her tightly against him. "You don't know what life is all about. You don't know what it's like to get kicked around, knocked down, get up, go get kicked again."

"I know how I feel about you. I love you. Nothing else mat- ters." Paul lowered his lips to her neck. Passion inflamed her, and she knew that if he stopped now, she would want to die. Aunt Lister had warned her of the hades fire that consumed the adulteress. Could anything be worth more than this? she wondered. Someone needing you, wanting you. And you are needing and wanting him also.

"I'll be back," she said to him when he kissed her goodbye. "I'll be back, but first I have to prove something to myself. Something to that little girl of long ago."

Chapter 3

....

MEMORIES

Back home again, Rachel relived her last night with Paul over and over again. She would stay for a while; she owed that to Aunt Lister. But then, she was going back to San Francisco and Paul. Each day passed as if stamped: breakfast was waiting when she awakened. After breakfast, she helped with the housework. In the afternoons, she took a long walk, played the piano, or tried to paint.

Out of loneliness, she made a game out of seeking Wilkins, strolling along the fields until he stopped for lunch.

Wilkins stepped from the reaper and dipped into the creek for a drink of water. His damp shirt clinging to him as his straw hat rested on the back of his head, showing dark curly hair drawn into clusters of curls by the perspiration.

Lowering herself, she sat on the sunbaked hay. Wilkins tossed his hat a few feet away and sat beside her.

"Haven't had much chance to talk to you alone," he said. Rachel flushed under his intense gaze.

"The city must have been good for you. You're looking mighty pretty these days," he said, caressing her arm with his fingers.

"Thank you," she said. "You're looking good too."

A big hand closed tightly over hers, and she caught her breath. This was a man she had known all her life. The boy of fifteen who carried her around on his shoulders. The memory grew strong, and she squeezed his hand. When she glanced up, Lister was coming toward them carrying Wilkins's lunch.

"We're in for a long hard winter," Lister said as she took sandwiches from the basket, pointing to the woods that skirted the field. "The leaves are falling early, and look! See how high that bees' nest is? Snow's going to be deep."

Dried leaves crunched in Rachel's hand. "I wonder if it's going to be cold in Frisco this winter. I'm going back in a few weeks."

Several weeks later, Rachel was still in Wymans Creek.

San Francisco seemed further away, and she was aware of Wilkins watching her—his eyes seeking hers across the room.

"I'm going to take my bath," she said to Lister one evening, "I want to go to bed early. Do you mind if I don't visit with you in the library tonight?"

"Why should I mind? You have been looking rather tired. One has to be careful this time of year. An early fall cold is just as nasty to get rid of as a summer cold," Lister said concerned.

Rachel left the room, but she heard Lister explaining her absence to Wilkins.

"I think Rachel is sickly. She's been so quiet and withdrawn— not herself at all. Do you think?" Lister's voice faded as Rachel reached the well.

The wooden bucket was heavy, and Rachel strained on the rope. Part of the water spilled back into the well. She carried the half-filled bucket into the summer house, emptying the water into the copper boiler on the stove. Pail after pail, she withdrew the water from the well. Wilkins stepped to her side. "I'd have gladly drawn the water for you—you aren't too grown up for me to do that." He took the bucket from her and lowered it into the well. She followed after him into the summer house.

The lamps in the library were glowing. Lister had retired for the evening and was reading.

Wilkins had changed from work overalls into plain white shirt and suit trousers. His face was closely shaven.

Paul's memory erased, and history repeated an experience of another time—a knowledge she knew existed and would seek forever to appease.

As he kissed her on her mouth, he held her from him. "I know how it is with you, Rachel."

Rachel nodded, the shame still with her.

"I watched you from the first time your Ma dumped you off. You had skinny legs, but I could tell you liked me even then. Teasing, even when you were a kid."

"That's not true."

"You know so well it's true. But I married Mary. I thought I wouldn't be thinkin' about you anymore. But it was worse. I lay awake at nights thinking about you."

Rachel viewed him coolly. "I loved a man in Frisco, a married man. I wanted to keep myself pure for the man I would marry some- day, but I remembered how you used to make me feel. From that day, I've been no better than the things they say about Mama."

"No, Rachel, you were cursed. You're a loose woman like your Ma. But I don't care. I was the first and I'll be the last."

"You'll be the last," she said, feeling the content of her words.

He left her standing in the center of the floor. She wanted to cry, but her tears seemed to be locked inside her.

"Wilkins is right," she brooded, "I am like Mama."

Her body was changing. For the past several weeks, she had felt more sensitive. There was a swelling and hard roundness to her abdomen. Her heart pounded! This explained her feeling out of sorts. Her lack of appetite. Her upset stomach. Morning sickness…

Another life was growing inside of her. *Paul's baby—oh my! How could I have been so blind not to know? How could I let the calendar pass me by and not know? I'm having Paul's baby,* saying she was sorry to Wilkins even though he was not there to hear her confession. A towel hung over a chair and she reached for it. Blackness shut out all light.

Lister was hovering over her when she awakened on the divan in the parlor.

"You fainted. Wilkins will fetch Dr. Stein. Why didn't I call the doctor sooner?" Lister said to Wilkins who was standing in the background, looking pale and frightened.

"I don't know, Mother." It was the first time Rachel ever heard him call Lister Mother.

Rachel sat up, holding her hand to her head. "I'm all right—it was so hot in there. I'm not sick. Really, I'm OK."

Several hours later, Dr. Stein arrived. The doctor had a slightly rounded stomach, protruding like a fat jolly elf. He put his hat on the table, then sat on the edge of the divan, reaching for her hand.

"Fast pulse," he said putting his hand to her head. "Don't have a fever, looks like the picture of health. Pretty little thing," he said, pinching her cheek roguishly.

Rachel looked down, embarrassed.

"When was your last period? Have you felt sick to your stomach in the morning?" Questions flew at her. Lister was in the room, and she couldn't answer him.

"These young'uns grow up so fast, can't keep up with them.

Don't recall an invite to her wedding."

Rachel's gasp aroused his suspicions, and he felt of her forehead again. "Could be the grip," he said, looking in scrutiny at Wilkins.

Wilkins left the room.

"Better check her over good," the doctor said, noting he had caused some confusion in the household. "These young women get embarrassed having an old man look them over, but I better make sure that it isn't catching."

Rachel's eyes expressed appreciation. The doctor walked Lister toward the kitchen.

"Would you like some tea and cakes when you've finished with Rachel, Doctor?"

"Lister, you always know the way to a man's heart," he said jestfully.

Lister Wyman giggled as the doctor left for further probing.

Dr. Joseph Stein closed the door to the parlor. Rachel clutched at the small quilt trying to cover her body. But at that moment, the doctor was more concerned with the happenings on the outside, looking out of the window, watching as snowflakes whirled geomet- rical designs that made little splashes against the window, melting at the impact.

The little round glasses the doctor wore made him look odd. Stranger yet, when he took a pipe from his pocket and lit it, placing it between lips that looked almost as fat as he was.

Wilkins helped her make a snowman one time. They put a big pumpkin on it for a head and a corn cob pipe into the place for the mouth. The snowman looked friendly—the doctor looked that way now.

"It's going to be a hard winter," he said. "Isn't the first of October yet and we're already tasting the first snow. It won't stay, but it's here, paving the way for the bitter snow that's bound to come."

Rachel didn't reply. *I won't be going to Frisco.* As if the doctor had read her thoughts he asked, "Does the young man know?"

Rachel's chin quivered. "No, he doesn't know. He won't ever know."

Dr. Stein drew the curtain closed, shutting out the snow flurry. "There's been a lot of young ladies in your predicament, but once the ceremony is over, it's forgotten. Time has healing powers."

"I said he'll never know."

"He isn't from around here, then?" Rachel shook her head. "No."

A sad look appeared on the doctor's face. "Did you love him?"

Rachel's eyes met his. "I loved him, but he already had a wife." The doctor knocked the ashes from his pip into the cuspidor.

"Rachel, I've lived a long time. I've seen a lot of girls in trouble. Some go away a few months—to school or to visit a relative. A few marry some other man. And I've seen some pretty girls grow into bitter old hags. I don't want that to happen to you."

He rubbed at his chin, and a philosophical look appeared in his eyes. "It's something special to be a woman. To house life in a body is a miracle. Some man would give his eye teeth to have you and claim that baby as his own. Even at my age, I get to thinking that if I found me a young woman, I'd feel virile again."

Rachel listened to the doctor, then she dropped back to the couch weary from the thoughts mulling through her mind.

Dr. Stein puffed frantically on his pipe. "Then, you might think about this—adoption."

A frightened gasp came from Rachel's lips. "Never, my mother gave me away. I'd never leave my baby. Not ever." Tears started to fall, and the pudgy man tried to console her.

"Lister's going to have one big fit. You can hide it for a while, but soon, you'll be bigger than a watermelon."

"I'll have to tell her," she said, sobbing. "She'll hate me like she does Mama. But I'll have to tell her."

"We'll tell her together. I am wondering if it isn't time that woman be taught the cold facts of life. You know, if she'd lived a little when she was younger wouldn't be such a dried-up old prune now. No, sir!" he guffawed.

Rachel blushed at the doctor's brusque manner, but she felt a closeness to him. He was someone she could trust.

Later, joining Lister and Wilkins in the kitchen, the doctor seemed at ease, helping himself to the cupcakes on the tea cart. He dropped two cubes of sugar into his tea, stirring briskly. "Nothing serious, nothing nature can't handle."

Lister appeared anxious. "I'll keep her in bed a couple days. I think all the excitement of the city was too much. You know, Doctor, she has a painting in the gallery already."

"Another artist?" the doctor cleared his throat. "There was a time when you were in Paris. Everyone figured you'd make yourself a name. Fooled all of us when you married old Rex."

"What you are saying, Doctor, is you always figured I was cut out for an old maid. You always had a biting tongue. You haven't changed one bit."

He reached for another cupcake and poured more hot water in his cup. "How old were you when you studied in Paris?"

Lister looked surprised. "Seventeen—maybe closer to eighteen. Why?"

"Rachel is twenty. I'd say that's a good age to start a family."

Lister looked shocked. "Are you trying to tell me that Rachel is in the family way?"

"Seven, eight weeks along. Now, Lister, don't you go harping at her. She needs understanding—a heap of it."

Lister eyed Wilkins suspiciously. "How could you? I raised you like brother and sister."

Wilkins dropped his arms to his side, glancing at Lister with a hopeful expression on his face.

"It's not mine. But I'll marry her if she'll have me."

The doctor fastened his leather bag, getting ready to leave. "Bless you, son. No one will be the wiser, if the wedding's within the next few weeks," he said, reaching for Wilkins's hand.

That night, Lister came to Rachel's room, drawing the shades, sitting beside her.

"I'm sorry, Auntie, I didn't want to hurt you. Please don't be angry with me. I loved him, Aunt Lister, I loved him with all my heart," she sobbed.

"I'm not angry with you. I blame myself. I didn't know how to tell you about men. The wiles they use to make young and innocent girls fall into their traps. Your mama was wild, but, Rachel, I know you aren't like she was. I know that!"

Lister tucked the covers up over Rachel's chest, then sat silently by her until she had stopped crying. How could she judge Rachel? Paris, over thirty years ago, she came home carrying a child. Rex mar- ried her. But Rex had Wilkins, nine years old. He needed a mother, and Rex married her. The marriage was good.

The child was stillborn. Lister placed her hand over the flabby muscles of her abdomen. The touch was soft, for the womb was vacant. Yet even now, she could feel the quickening. She took Rex Wyman's name, but she never gave love.

Love belonged to another time, another place, another man. The next morning, Wilkins came to Rachel's room. He was clean shaven and wearing his Sunday suit.

"Rachel," he said softly, "I'll marry you now if you want."

She was stirred and struggled with desire to offer herself to him. "I'll have to think about it. I can't answer you now. I can't let you pay for my mistake."

Squaring his jaw as he saw the longing in her eyes, content to wait for her decision. Knowing someday he would obtain the prize. A few days before the wedding, Rachel wrote Paul. *It's as if I never loved him at all,* she thought. *One word of love and I'll go to him.*

Sniffing the tears she felt, she wrote:

Dear Paul,

I am very happy. I will be married shortly.

Thank you for the wonderful time in San Francisco.

Several weeks later, a reply came. A short note and a portrait he had painted of her.

She read the letter out loud, as if the unborn child might understand.

"Congratulations are in order, although I find it hard to write. Happiness is all I can wish for you. Do not neglect your painting. Of all my students you have genuine talent. I would like to see you try other mediums, perhaps pastels. Write me sometime, Rachel."

The signature, Paul, was signed lightly, the L fading into a lengthy line.

"Paul," she whispered, "my poor lonely Paul."

Guilt ridden for her forbidden desires, she pressed the letter to her lips. *I have destroyed a love that was surely made in Heaven.* Blandly, she bypassed the thought. *Perhaps, it only existed in my per- sonal hades— that's where my sins are headed.*

A book lay on the bedside table, and she placed the letter between the pages. Still holding the book, she walked to the balcony window. Overhead clouds gathered black and threatening. Her mar- riage to Wilkins flitted through her mind. An empty parlor, a drab dress. A minister from Clarmourne. Dr. Stein and Aunt Lister, the only guests. Flowers were absent. Frost had nibbled on the last of the roses. Shattered dreams.

A wedding day as dark and dismal as the sadness carefully guarded inside of her.

The next day, it started to snow.

Chapter 4

MARRIAGE

S now fell night and day for nearly a week, banking with a forceful wind. Virtually snowbound, the mail was not deliv- ered; groceries and household needs were hauled in on a sled.

Rachel spent the lonely days playing the piano and secretly praying for another letter from Paul. It was only a dream for she knew his pride. There would never be another letter. Her marriage to Wilkins had forfeited that right.

Wilkins was understanding of Rachel's condition, not forcing his rights as a husband. Throughout the long nights, they lay side by side, no part of their physical bodies touching. It was agony for Rachel, hearing his deep sighs of longing. She wished to touch him and needed caresses. Wilkins wanted his husband's rights for satisfac- tion that come with Marriage. But making love was void and cold. Days passed, then weeks, and months. The birth of the child neared, and physical contact was cut off because of pride, fear, and guilt.

In desperation, Rachel tried to fill the emptiness by experiment- ing with every medium Paul taught her. Useless creative efforts. Hours spent trying to record the beauty of winter on canvas. Distorted and ugly in her mind, she failed to capture the scene her eyes saw. Angry at her imperfections, she threw the canvas into the fire, weeping when the flames devoured it. Her dream of becoming a great artist dimmed that winter.

Wilkins, in his misery, spent more time in Wymans Creek. The saloon became a solace and Rachel became a stranger.

Their eyes seldom meeting and their hands never touching.

Rachel nurtured the thought of having a child, holding and crooning to it. A baby is the offspring of two people.

The baby was all hers now, and soon, it would also belong to Wilkins.

The baby would soon have the Wyman name.

Winter passed, slowly and remorsefully. Then as if to change the pace of short days and long nights, spring came in the budding of the willow and brilliant splashes of color as Lister's tulips and daf- fodils bloomed. March entered like a lion and disappeared into April as gentle as the woolly lamb of the almanac's prediction. But April is also in the sign of the Ram; the case in which it entered was in for- bearance with the sign. Nights were clear and a full moon cast shim- mering lights on the new birth of green. Even the stars looked mag- nified and more brilliant. Winter was past. Frogs infested the creek, choral groups restless with melodious croaking. Everyone anticipated the baby to be born in the new season.

Rachel longed to see Paul in the baby's features. Wilkins wished for the birth for personal reasons; Lister waited anxiously, solely to assure her that the Wyman name would pass to another generation. So the life within Rachel's body was urged to be born.

Everyone was waiting—each having an apparent selfish and deliberate motive.

Then April proved a traitor to her tradition. It started snowing in late afternoon, and by dinnertime, snow covered the ground again. Lister retired to the library and picked up her sewing. Rachel remained at the dinner table, fidgety and uncomfortable suffering from the first pangs of childbirth. Wilkins, unaware of her pain, left to change into his dark striped suit and dress shirt. He was making his regular Saturday night visit to Wyman's Creek Saloon. Perspiration dripped from her brow as she nervously collected the dishes and car- ried them into the kitchen. The water was boiling, and she poured it into the pan, waiting for it to cool before dropping the dishes in it. Wilkins came down the stairway, and she wanted to beg him not to go. He smelled like shaving lotion, and she felt sick to her stomach. She had never asked him not to go, but now she felt strange and fear-

ful. What if her baby would come when he was gone?

What if it was coming right now? There were things like false labor pains and she'd never had a baby before. How could she tell false pains from the real ones? *Please, God, don't let him go tonight,* she prayed.

"I don't think you should go into town tonight," she said as he reached for his mackinaw.

"Why in the World not?"

"It's snowing hard—might be a violent storm, maybe a blizzard."

The door slammed. Pacing back and forth between the window and the door, she was unable to rest. Through the window, it looked as if an artist had taken a pencil and sketched an outline of silver over the darkness of the foliage. Dusk deepened, and she could scarcely see the bridge. A jagged pain knifed her lower back. Her time had come. With each pain, she felt the desire to abort—to forever remove the object that was a burden inside of her. She frantically pounded on the library door.

"My goodness, Rachel." Lister opened the door. "You should have told me, have you timed the pains?"

Rachel shook her head. "It just hurts so much—"

"Don't worry, Rachel, just rest while I go for Dr. Stein." Lister quickly draped a shawl over her shoulders. "Don't bear down. I'll be back as soon as I can."

Wilkins had taken the team; that left only the bay. Blanketing the horse quickly, she led it over the bridge as it shimmied and shied over the slippery boards. With only a kerosene lantern for light, she tried following Wilkins's fading wagon tracks.

"Lister?" the old doctor answered the door, trying to fasten his pants. "You look like you've seen a ghost."

"It's Rachel, she's in labor, started at dinner time. The pains are hard and coming close."

"We'll tie your mare in the barn," he said, struggling with his boots. "Grab my overcoat."

Frantically fighting for time, they trampled through drifts to the barn. Lister held the lantern while he harnessed the team.

"I don't know what I'd do if anything happened to her, she's like my own daughter."

"Don't get all riled," Dr. Stein said calmly. "It's her first. They take a little more time getting here, she'll be fine."

True to the doctor's word, they arrived to find Rachel in a surprisingly happy spirit. Agonizing pains made her gasp, but she smiled when she saw the doctor.

"Just in the nick of time," he said, examining her.

There was no desire to fight the weariness when the chloro- form-saturated handkerchief was held over Rachel's nose and mouth. Distant muddled voices droned. Someone was crying and moan- ing, but as the pain dimmed, so did her other senses. A cutting pain released the child, and she felt it slipping from her body, realizing she had heard her own cries. Then she felt so tired.

"Looks like a big fellow," the doctor mused, as he slapped the child gently on the buttocks. At the child's vigorous wails, Rachel fought for consciousness as the doctor anxiously awaited the first signs of the expulsion of the afterbirth. Noting the time of arrival, Dr. Stein jotted down the figures on the back of a receipt he had in his shirt pocket. "Baby boy Wyman, born 5:30 a.m. April 14, 1923," Knitting his eyebrows in concentration, he scribbled in "6 lbs. more or less."

Lister questioned the blondness of the baby as she washed and dressed him, wishing he resembled the Wymans with their black hair and blue eyes. She pondered over that awhile, but the child so innocent and weak aroused an instinct in Lister. Holding the baby close to her breast, she forgot it did not belong to her.

"Keep her in bed for at least a week and let me know if she has any trouble. Otherwise, I'll stop by next Tuesday. Got to check on the old woman anyway."

Lister held her finger gently to her lips, cautioning the doctor to leave quietly. Dr. Stein grumbled, then let himself out the door.

Chapter 5

WILKINS ACCIDENT

D r. Stein drove the team toward the Wyman Creek bridge. It was a beautiful morning, the snow crusted and shimmering as the sun melted it with the Swiftness of a Chinook.

Chunks of ice crashed from the trees, sometimes taking branches with it.

The doctor was in a mysterious mood. He had assisted in a miracle, the dawning of a new life. After delivery, he always felt a surge of God's power. As a doctor, he was an instrument by which the Lord worked.

Wilkins was a burden to him, tomcatting around when he was to become a father. Not by blood lines, but a sacred trust when he accepted the responsibilities of marriage to Rachel.

Suddenly, it occurred to him that the horses Wilkins drove to town were not tied when he saw them munching on some straw pawed out from under the snow. Slowly, cautiously, premonitorily, he stopped his team just short of a hump that lay slush covered on the bridge.

The railing was dangling over the side. A branch from the wil- low tree had been dragged along the road. How it nearly covered the form.

"Whoa, Bell, whoa, Bess." He jumped from the wagon seat with the audacity of a man younger than his sixty odd years. There was no mistaking the curly black hair and the red and white macki- naw. It was Wilkins. Frantically, the doctor clawed at the debris until his fingers felt numb. Baring Wilkins's chest, a heartbeat so faint and weak, but Wilkins was alive.

The wagon lay broken on its side, blocking the road, wheels fro- zen in their axles. He marveled that Wilkins was thrown free instead of lying beneath the mangled mess.

Dr. Stein always felt small in comparison to Wilkins. Now he was a giant! Wilkins was stiff and solid, but inch by inch, the doctor raised the big man until he lay stumped in the rear of the wagon.

Lister watched the strange maneuvering of the doctor.

When she saw him back the team from the bridge and turn around, she ran out to meet him.

"Give me a hand, Lister," Dr. Stein said as he tried to lift Wilkins from the wagon. "He's froze nearly to death. Lucky he's preserved in alcohol."

Lister cringed at the doctor's words. It was not that she did not know of Wilkins's indulgences in Wymans Creek, but it wounded her pride that the doctor was also aware of it.

"Should I heat some water for a bath?" she asked.

"Goodness no! He'll have to thaw out slow or the shock will kill him." He draped his coat over a chair and tossed his little round hat on the divan. "Any heat now will only add to his misery."

Opening his bag, he took a bottle of whiskey from it. "Don't know if this will help," he said, pouring some into Wilkins's mouth. "Might keep him quiet when he starts thawing out. Chillblains are tougher than hades."

He yanked at the boots on Wilkins's feet, letting them fall hard on the floor. Woolen socks clung stubbornly, and the doctor cut them off with Lister's sewing shears. Wilkins's feet were discolored and lifeless.

"It's too late, isn't it?" Lister asked with a sob in her throat.

Thoughts raced back and forth in the doctor's mind. He couldn't answer that. He was all too aware of the complications of frostbite.

Wilkins was conscious and tried to speak but made only moan- ing sounds. Pins and needles were doing a dance in his hands, but his legs and feet were lifeless.

So much in one day, the doctor thought as he stepped out onto the porch. A decision must be made. He took his pipe from his pocket and filled it with tobacco, cursing when he discovered he had lost his matches. The sky was clear and cloudless, the rising sun so bright he had to close his eyes. "God, today you seem so far away, but I know you're up there somewhere. You know what I have to do. Seems everything that happens there is some kind of a balance. Today, I escorted a new life into this world. Now, I have to make up my mind if I want to lose a life or destroy a man. Being a medical man, don't have much choice. So, Lord, I'll do my job, but I need some help."

Dr. Stein took a few deep breaths, then he went back into the library to face his task.

"Heat some water," he ordered.

Lister looked at him, questioning. "Oh man! Should I awaken Rachel?"

The doctor shook his head. "No, she'll know soon enough."

Never in all the years of his practicing had he ever performed an amputation. Now, he was going to have to do a double one, and he didn't know if he had the guts to do it.

He tried to force some more whiskey down Wilkins, then took a long swallow himself. His patient was a drinking man and the alco- hol did not have the effect the doctor wished for.

Some of the chloroform he had used for the delivery was still in his case, and he sighed with relief. Wilkins grappled, then surrendered.

Over sterile gauze and clean sheets, Dr. Stein performed his bloodiest and most dreaded surgery. Beads of perspiration trickling down into the deep crevices of his face. Many times, his hands fal- tered, but he worked steady without rest.

Wilkins's face showed tormented contortions. More chloroform was held over his face.

"Good girl," Dr. Stein praised Lister, as he washed the blood from his hands and arms.

Lister started to weep, and the doctor felt guilty watching the woman who appeared so strong break down.

"I had to do it, Lister. I don't think I did that man a favor. There just wasn't a choice. Sometimes, I wish I had been a butcher like my old man instead of a doctor. You know, Lister, there's not that much difference."

He rinsed off the instruments and put them back into his case. Exhausted, he sat down into the rocker in front of the fire. The rocker creaked back and forth, but there was no rest for him. *It's so quiet,* he reflected. As quiet as death. Then he heard the new baby cry and the animalistic groans of Wilkins. Neither the babe nor the man was aware of his existence.

The doctor wondered how the newborn infant must feel to all of a sudden have to force air into his lungs to even breathe. Wilkins, used to having the advantages of a whole man, to awaken in a hostile world with no mode for travel. A man who had walked the fields behind a plow, whose whole lifestyle depended upon his ability to use his legs. What would his reactions be when he discovered that he was only half a man?

And what of Rachel? A young wife and a new mother. What would her new world be like? Awakening from the exhausted post- natal sleep to discover she was responsible for a new man-child and bound to a legless creature depending upon her for his every need.

God help her! he surmised, reviewing the rehabilitation of other amputees. How many times does a big virile man like Wilkins find that he is impotent?

A chill gathered around him, and he tasted fear in his mouth.

It's already began—this house is taking on the vibrations of this family. He looked at Lister asleep in a chair, holding Rachel's baby in her arms. Doctor Stein lifted the baby from her arms and took him into Rachel. She opened her eyes when he placed the baby next to her.

"Is it a boy?" she asked happily. "Big whopper, six pounds," he said.

Rachel unwrapped the baby, carefully inspecting the tiny feet and hands. "He's beautiful!" she said with a radiant beam.

"I'm going to name him Rex Paul. Rex after Wilkins's father, and—"

"And Paul after his father," the doctor interrupted.

Rachel smiled, holding the child to her breast, drifting back into her dream world—a world safe from external happenings. Strolling through a grassy park and Paul was holding her close.

The shade of the window was partially open, and from where Wilkins was lying, he could see the sun's rays beating through the frost. Cutting the pattern into a stream of water steadily dripping down the window pane. Sliding onto the already stained wallpaper.

Drop by drop, it ran into a little stream that hit the floor and made a puddle.

The warmth of the sun made a bare spot on the window pane, and he felt the heat across his body. He tried to move out of its way, but he couldn't.

How did he get into the library? He was lying on the sewing table, and it was hard as cement.

Must have really hung one on last night, he thought, watching the fire in the fireplace spit orange and yellow daggers against the screen. His legs wouldn't move.

He traced the night in Wymans Creek in his mind. A horrible blizzard—snow so thick he couldn't see his hands in front of his face. The wind blowing, building the snow across the town in lopsided drifts.

He was sitting in the tavern, drinking straight whiskey with water for a chaser. A woman sitting beside him, caressing him. A hotel room, it smelled musty. The woman was laughing, and they drank some more. She went to sleep before anything could happen. Had to get home. Had to feed the stock.

The snow had stopped, but drifts piled one on another.

Couldn't see the bridge. The bridge—he remembered! Now, he was laying stiff and solid on Lister's sewing table.

Through the window, he could see the snow sliding down the roof. In big chunks it fell, crashing as it hit the ground. Naked as a jaybird, sweat poured from him, and how he ached. His legs throbbed, and he couldn't budge them. *Maybe I drank some rotten whiskey.* He kept reliving the scenes over and over in his mind.

Wasn't much of a woman, but I can't touch Mary.

Cold as a hunk of ice she's having a baby. I keep hearing a baby cry. No, it's not Mary—it's Rachel. Oh my! I'm so sick, my guts are rolling inside of me. Everything is spinning, round and round. I've got to get the out of here, got to throw hay down to the stock. Somebody help me. I'm stuck to this table like glue.

"Somebody help me!"

No one answered him. *I heard Dr. Stein talking. He gave me some whiskey, he held something over my nose. I couldn't breathe. He tried to kill me! I married Rachel, and now they want me dead. They want to squander all the money away my old man left. Art lessons—this place can go to hades, but they have to have their culture.*

"Oh man," he wept. "I wanted Rachel, it was like a sickness. I can't touch her. Some man in Frisco. I can't even feel amorous toward her, she's like her Ma." *My legs, they feel like they're rotted to the bone.*

I'm thirsty, someone give me a drink. The sun is so hot and my legs— my legs? Wilkins ran his hand down his thigh and his fingers stopped.

"What happened to my legs?" he yelled. "You dirty butcher, you chopped off my legs. You can't cut a tree down and stick it back in the dirt. No more legs are going to grow back on me."

Dr. Stein heard Wilkins curse, and he sat beside him, holding him like a father comforts a son.

"Son," he said. "We had to do it."

"My word," Wilkins whimpered. "I'm not even a whole man."

April brought one new life and one life destroyed. The baby adjusted normally and grew in his new surroundings, for the mother's love was as potent on the outside world as in the Shell. For Wilkins, it was a different matter; the world was cruel and calculating. He refused to be pitied and, like an injured animal, snapped at anyone who held out a kind hand.

Rachel tried to make up for his loss by playing the piano for him and reading his favorite Westerns out loud. Lister spent her time in the kitchen preparing dishes she thought would please him. Before the baby's birth, Rachel and Wilkins were strangers.

Now, they were not even that. Rachel nursed his wounds and unconsciously cringed at the sight of his blanketed stubs. Throughout the long nights, she sat by his side, comforting him as nightmares haunted him. In his misery, he begged for whiskey. She obliged him. It made him more tranquil.

When the doctor warned him about his dependency on alco- hol, Wilkins cursed. "What in the world do I care? When I'm half tanked, I can't think."

Dr. Stein tried to explain the needs of Rachel and their son. Words, to Wilkins, were vacant, dangling expressions, and he refused to listen.

Chapter 6

REALITY SETS IN

T he years pass swiftly in a house reeking with the stench of death. Wilkins was dying a slow death advocated by self-pity and remorse. Rachel was dying of loneliness, for a woman without a man's love is already accustomed to the grave. Lister received her sentence to death when Dr. Stein found a malignancy growing within her, expanding soon to encompass her whole intes- tine. Lister was silent in her condemnation to doom, accepting each day as it arrived. She harbored an earnest sense of God's reckoning and sought her Bible daily for proof of man's immortality. If she should perish, it was consoling to know that her blood lines would flow on in the veins of her kin.

Amid the obscurity, a ray of hope existed in the young boy. Rachel viewed Rex Paul as somewhat of a miracle, inheriting his blond handsomeness from Paul, but he had acquired her sensitivity, her delicate hands, and the excitability of the Lansing temperament. Rex Paul was a brilliant child, and though his eagerness entertained Rachel, it was often a source of irritability to Wilkins. But he had the patience to overlook a bad temper. The snow had again been heavy the previous winter. Surrounding knolls still shrouded by a cloak of fine sifted talc, glazed brittle by icy winds.

With the coming of the new moon, warm, dry breezes coddled the valley. With the warmth came destruction. Gigantic portions of the hillside thundered onto the Wyman ranch.

The creek flooded, leaving the willow tree, branches dipped in mud, as the only reminder of the beautiful gardens and lower grain fields.

Although, murky, slimy water slammed the underside, the bridge stood remarkably sturdy. The house was an island, a lonely sentinel roughly embraced by ripped branches, roots, and silt that seemed to follow a route mapped by some unruly hand. Were it not for the knoll on which the house was built, it may also have been devoured by the ravenous and revenge spring upheaval.

As the sun came out again, the house itself regained activity. Rachel wrapped a blanket around the mutilated limbs of Wilkins, and Lister tossed her shawl over her shoulders.

Together, they went outside to review the damages. Lister wailed over the loss of her flower beds and the sick condition of the lawn. Wilkins cursed as he remembered that he had once raised the best grain in the valley. Rachel seemed immune to tears. The sun was shining again, but only time and a new rain could wash away the filth.

"John Erickson said he would like to put the crops in on shares again," Lister said to Wilkins. "It's not too late for a silage crop, and—"

"The seeds ruined. Don't make much sense just sitting here rotting." Wilkins gazed across the field. "Good thing we sold the stock. Should sell the whole place."

"I wouldn't think of selling," Lister said. "Your father waxed good from this ranch and his father before him. Someday Rex Paul can farm it."

"I hope I never live to see it," Wilkins said. Lister pretended she hadn't heard Wilkins reply.

"Things aren't bad yet. I still have some of your father's insur- ance money. It'll be enough to see us through the year and, God will- ing, enough to bury me." Lister added with a wistful glance toward Rex Paul who was wandering toward the creek.

"Bury you?" Wilkins said with fear. "You'll be around for a long time."

Rachel shivered. "Auntie, it's a sin to talk like that! You've been working too hard."

Lister knelt down to lift a broken rose bush, then she said sadly, as if comparing her condition to that of the rose. "Guess old age doesn't have any guarantees. When my time comes, I'll be ready."

"You aren't old," Rachel said. "Why, you're only sixty, are you sixty yet? Grandma Lansing was nearly eighty when she died."

"Sixty is old for some people. And I'm old. I raised you and Wilkins, and I've lived long enough to see a Wyman heir."

The sun dipped behind a cloud, and the brilliance of the day faded with it. Rachel watched concerned as Lister walked slowly back toward the house.

"Do you think Aunt Lister is sick?" Rachel asked Wilkins.

"I'd say she's getting senile. Reading her Bible all night, still gets up with the chickens."

"See, Mama!" Rex Paul called as he poked at the swirling foam with a small willow switch. Deep in thought about Lister, Rachel glanced briefly toward her child, then followed Lister to the house. There was a frightened shriek as Rex Paul tumbled into the already riled water. Wilkins speeded toward the bridge in his wheelchair, reaching it in time to hold out his hand to the struggling child. Rex Paul was safe on the bridge. Wilkins's chair started to roll, and before Rachel reached him, the chair and Wilkins were in the water.

"Rex Paul," she said to the dripping child. "Get Aunt Lister. Daddy fell in the water. Hurry!"

Rachel tore her shoes from her feet and dove into the cluttered water. She was not a strong swimmer and realized the hopelessness of trying to rescue an invalid.

"Try and float," she commanded as she neared him. He kept threshing around as if trying to avoid her.

"Keep your head above water," she ordered. He was being dragged away with the current, and she strained her muscles trying to reach him. Tears blinded her eyes, but she clutched at his shirt with one hand, reaching for the dangling bridge railing with the other. His shirt ripped, and she felt him slip away from her.

Please God, she prayed silently, *I've got to help him.* She reached for his suspenders, and he jerked away from her.

"Let me help you," she pleaded. "I need you, Aunt Lister needs you."

A sensuous pleasure crossed his face as he outfought her maneuvers. Calculating her next action, she swam in behind him, holding his suspenders. He started to sink, and she let his face emerge in the water. When he quit struggling, she towed him toward shore.

He was limp and breathless, but she found the strength to turn him over and raise his arms above his head.

"Curse you!" he said. "Rachel, curse you."

"Oh, thank God, thank God you're alive. Wilkins," she wept, "you're letting that accident make your mind sick."

He coughed and spit. "If I'm crazy, it's because I see how you look at me. I see how other men look at you."

"That's not true," she said, holding him in her arms.

"It's true, all right, you know well it's true. I'm crazy, but it's because you won't let me be a whole man."

Covered with mud and slime, they were clinging to each other. "You shut me out, you won't even let me touch you," Rachel wept. "You won't even let me sleep with you."

When Lister arrived with John Erickson, they were both weeping.

It was late afternoon before Dr. Stein came.

"You're tough as all nails," he said to Wilkins. "But that was one fool stunt."

"Don't lecture me, Doc. I wanted out! Almost made it."

The doctor's face set in a hard-grimaced pose. "You wanted out! Let me tell you something. You don't give one care for anyone except yourself, sitting around sucking on a bottle of booze all day. Rachel is gnawing her soul out for you, and you let Lister wait on you hand and foot. Have you ever given it a thought? For that matter have you ever given a second thought about anything except yourself?"

"You don't know what it's like," Wilkins whined, "to be half a man."

"Half a man? Who in the world do think you are? Do you think you're the only one who's suffered? It's high time you grow up, son.

Lister won't be around much longer, and it's time you stand on your own two feet. I could cut my tongue out for saying that!"

Dr. Stein jabbed his pipe into his mouth not bothering to light it. "Got to get along. Lister will be in bed a good share of the time. Try and make her life a little easier, dying isn't easy."

"Dying?" Wilkins asked. "Can't you give her something? You're the doctor—she can't die."

"She's dying, Wilkins. Cancer, someday it may be as easy as that—a cure. But now, it's a blessing when death comes."

"She's in the same boat as I'm in," Wilkins said.

"Hardly," the doctor flashed a look of pity at Wilkins. "There's a big difference. Lister treasures life, you don't give one hoot for yours."

The doctor walked to the door. "It's this house," he muttered to himself. He reached for the door knob, then stalled as if he had forgotten something and went into the library.

Lister and Rachel were busily sewing a garment for Rex Paul. The boy lay on the Chesterfield striking an impish pose. "How's the young man?" the doctor asked.

"Tell Dr. Stein how you feel," Rachel coached.

"I fell in the water, Daddy fell in too. Will Daddy's chair drown?"

"Won't hurt the chair any but listen to me. That creek can be mighty mean in the spring, stay clear of it, hear?"

"I think he's learned his lesson," Rachel said, then added with a frightened look in her eyes. "Doctor, Wilkins didn't want me to help him."

He patted her gently on the arm. "I know, I've been pretty harsh with him. Go help that poor man. Though I can't pamper him, I know how he feels. He's more of a man than I can ever be—even with both legs bobbed."

For a while, the doctor seemed more interested in the pair of knickers Lister was hemming than in Lister's illness.

"You're one good seamstress," he pinched her jestfully on the cheek. "Still my girl?"

Lister's eyes met his. "I had an awful jolt today, but I guess I have a lot more misery ahead of me. Did you tell Wilkins?"

"I tried. It was good getting it off my chest. It may do some good, getting something else on his mind." He scratched at his chin. "Then again it might not, might be just one more kick in the pants." "I've been trying to prepare him for it. He's had such a hard life.

First losing his mother, then Mary died, on top of all that, his legs. Sometimes, it seems fate picks out certain people and strikes them down with all her fury."

Dr. Stein relit his pipe and his mind seemed to drift before he answered her.

"Naw, Lister, it just seems that way. Life is full of jolts. We can't grow until we've had our share. Wilkins just got a bigger share than most of us that's all. Now, take me, life looks rosy to someone from the outside. But it's lonely. A patient dies, I lose a friend. Each time something happens to one of them, I feel like it's happening to me. When Wilkins lost his legs, I was feeling like mine were rotting off.

"When I was in Medical School, they told us to remain imper- sonal toward our patients. But it doesn't work. When you've prac- ticed in one place all your life, it gnaws on you. Before you know it, you laugh when they laugh, and you bawl when they bawl. Lately, I've done my share of bawling."

Chapter 7

DR. STEIN AT HOME

The sharp odor of Lysol was still stinging his nose as Dr. Stein jumped on the carriage seat and grasped the reins of his team. Lister was one very good housekeeper, killing all those germs if only it would help Rachel and the boy. But the stinking that house was from a lot more than just booze and tobacco smoke. There was a sickness there, and all the medical knowledge in the world could not cure it.

He pulled his hat down over his brow and shut his eyes, leaving the team to reach the cottage by instinct.

The air was full of dampness, and the sun kept its hiding place behind the clouds. It would be one muddy mess if it rained again. The road felt lumpy as the wagon groaned over the gravel.

When the horses came to a halt, he pushed his hat roughly to the back of his head and reached for the leather bag on the seat.

He talked to the horses as he always did when he brushed them down and placed a bucket of oats before them. "Now one of these days I'll have one of them new automobiles, you nags will get your rest then." Laughing at the thought of riding swiftly over the roads leaving a cloud of dust behind him. Someday, when he had the money, but money was something he never worried too much about. Slumping wearily to the back entrance of his cottage, he pushed the thought out of his mind.

He stopped to split some wood for the fireplace and found the exertion made him short of breath. Well, one of these days, he'd leave his practice to the young doctors. All them new things coming up— cures for this and that. The old folk were still calling him, but the young ones were having their babies in the Clarmourne Hospital. Home deliveries just aren't fashionable anymore, and they are giving some new type of treatment for the carcinomas. New things in the Journal every issue. *Someday, I'll take time to study up on them.*

There was a gentle mew at his feet and he picked up the big tiger cat that had begun to nuzzle against his boot.

"What you want, Cat? Forget to give you your milk before I left?"

The cat squirmed as he grasped it, holding it close while he reached for the jar of milk kept cool on the north window ledge. He clumsily poured some milk into a dish, laughing heartily as the cat jumped from his arms to lap up the milk.

He poured some more milk into a cup for himself and sliced a chunk from a salami roll, slapping it over a thick piece of bread. *Wasn't like this when Julie was here,* he thought, there would be the smell of meat cooking—sometimes roast chicken or stuffed cabbages. When he was younger and out on house calls, he complimented the house-wives by tasting their culinary efforts—repaying them with a gentle pinch or a soft pat to their fat rumps. But that was when he was younger and before his prostrate bothered him. Now, he was having one awful time just to urinate. Yawning sleepily, the cat climbed to his lap. It had been a kitten when he had found it out on the back porch—a soft bundle of fur, wild, and nearly starved. He chuckled remembering how he had forced the cat's nose into the warmed milk; it shook its head and sneezed. That was four, maybe five years ago.

It was strange having an intruder in the house, but for the first time since Julie left, it was someone that was waiting for him to get home. He could talk to the cat and it was something to caress.

The castration was done when it was still a kitten.

No use having a cat around unless it earned its keep, he figured. He never bothered to seek a name for it. Just Cat. Cat grew into a big gorgeous hunk of "it" with yellow eyes and a hoarse mew that scared the dickens out of him when he wasn't thinking the cat was around.

So Cat was always there, and sometimes when he wasn't fumed up over one of his patients, he had the dreadful fear that someday he would come home, and Cat wouldn't be there.

It had been that way with Julie. A doctor's wife must take a lot of things that other wives aren't required to do. There are the late- night calls, the smell of death and sickness, and the terrible loneli- ness. Julie wasn't cut out for that. She was a lady straight through, but she was fickle.

She didn't give one iota if his patients needed him or not. Thirty years ago, he had come home from a delivery. The Wilde's baby— breech, and it was a tough one. He remembered walking through the door, calling her name. He found the note. Julie was gone. *Sometimes, I think I can still feel her hand on my arm—she always smelled so good, like lilacs in a bouquet. The smell of her stuck with you.*

Julie was his right arm, but then she was gone. He wrote and begged her to come back, but she didn't come home. And Julie destroyed the male in him just as surely as he had neutered the cat.

Cat gave out with one of his peculiar bellows and shifted his position. Dr. Stein stroked the smooth fur.

"Now, Cat, I tell you Lister is one good woman. She sure is set in her ways—stubborn as a mule, but goodness sake, that woman would give you the shirt off her own back."

The cat was purring, and the doctor kept talking to it. "Yep, she's done one wonderful job raising Rachel and Wilkins. Didn't bat an eyelash either when Rachel got in trouble. I thought for sure she'd have fits."

"And Wilkins, that poor man! Losing Lister won't help his atti- tude any. Not after what happened to Mary."

As Mary's doctor, he kept her secrets, all these years. He knew why Mary couldn't conceive. A rash of guilt surged through him, he had played God. How many times had he tampered with God's laws?

He was given the gift of healing, with that gift went an overdose of compassion. Mary was only fourteen and raped; he could not bear to see her suffer. So he performed the abortion. Didn't charge a nickel either. Never found out who the man was. Any medical man would have done the same thing, he always told himself. It was an awful truth to face for he always used that argument and he knew it was the vilest of lies.

"Iceberg," Wilkins complained. But Dr. Stein knew Mary's fears. No man ever used Mary again. She was twenty when she mar- ried Wilkins, and only twenty-three when she died. It was one of those nasty things that hit fast. By the time he got to her bedside, her lungs were filled with fluid. A person with a deep yearning to live would have made it. But Mary did not want to live; she still harbored the sense of self-hate. There was no fight in her because there was none to begin with.

Dr. Stein put the cat down onto the rug and stirred the dying coals in the fireplace. The fire spit and hissed as he dropped another log on it. Pitch oozed from the wood and the fire blazed brightly.

When he raised from the fireplace, there was the stabbing pain in his chest again. Angina—it was coming more frequent now. He put a nitroglycerine tablet under his tongue. The heat surged through his body, and he sat stiffly grasping the arms of the chair. The pain subsided, and he closed his eyes trying to doze. The dreaded fear of death torturing him.

Tomorrow, he thought, *I'll go to Clarmourne. Get one of them young whipper-snappers to take over my practice.*

They'll be brash, and they'll play games with God. Later they'll join hands with Him. First, they'll try everything they were taught in Medical School, only they'll discover you don't learn everything out of a book.

Medical know-how comes with practice and praying. Take Lister for instance—they will take her and put the knife to her. The cancer will spread all over her guts, but they will try to undo their mistakes by those fancy new treatments. Lister will die regardless of what they do. She'll die, but they may prolong her misery.

Lister will die, and I'll die. Our only hope is that the young doctors learn something from it. A lot of cures and treatments will be found, but a lot of people will die because they've been nothing but human guinea pigs.

And Wilkins doesn't have a leg to stand on. They will have him on wooden pegs and he will stumble all over the place forcing himself to move. When the irritation sets in a little more, it will be chopped off, and they'll start all over again.

Shaking, he tried to light his pipe. The bowl seemed unable to make contact with the match. *If I were a drinking man, I'd get drunk—can't tolerate the stuff. I'm all keyed up because I didn't learn somewhere back when I was teachable that I'm not a god. I shake like a willow-wisp just sitting around, but I'm calm as a day without a breeze when I'm working.*

Work is a deceiver. If I didn't have a patient to stew over, might as well be dead. I know how they feel and I know what they think. I work them over in my head and I ache with them.

The Lord says to live for just one day at a time.

Can't learn that either. Lister's dying, and I can see the heartache ahead for Rachel, and I bawl in my sleep when I dream about Wilkins.

The cat aroused him from his reverie with one of the fierce meows. The doctor opened the door to let the cat out.

"Don't you yowl at the door now, 'cause when I turn in, it will take a lot more noise than you can muster to wake me up."

With the cat springing into the darkness, Dr. Stein paused long enough to turn the cardboard sign to read, "Doctor Is Out." Pudgy fingers fumbled with the latch on the leather case. When it was opened, he dug to the bottom until he had all the fixings at hand: rubbing alcohol, syringe, sterilized water, and the tablets.

He took his coat off, then his shirt and trousers. Standing bulky and flabby in the fleece-lined underwear, he shoved the sleeve high on his left arm and dabbed at the bared flesh with the alcohol-satu- rated cotton ball. Then he placed the tablet in the syringe and stuck the needle into the rubber stop, drawing the water into the instru- ment. When the air was pushed out of the needle, he jabbed it into his arm.

The point of the needle broke through the skin and he felt the sting as the liquid was forced into his arm. Quickly, he pulled the needle out and held another piece of cotton over the pin-point hole. The syringe was dropped into the enameled pan with the other uten- sils of the day.

It would take but a few minutes before the drug took effect, so he hurried with his bedtime chores, anxiously awaiting unencum- bered sweet sleep. He puffed frantically on his pipe, then knocked the ashes into the fireplace, crowding the heavy screen in closer to the fire.

Ready for bed, he attempted to empty his bladder into the bed- side chamber. He had come to dread this one necessary chore. *New blood!* he thought, lying heavily upon the bed, pulling the wool blan- ket over him, feeling the effects of the drug. Only hope in new blood. There was a whirling sensation and he was floating gently, fan- cying that Julie was lying beside him, her soft body bared against him.

"Julie," he whispered her name.

He started to rumble on the happenings of the day and Julie was lost again—faded out by the moaning and groanings of the peo- ple he knew and loved the best. There were some that called him Doc and then, there were some who called him a quack.

Chapter 8

DR. GERALD BONLEY THE NEW PRACTITIONER

Dr. Gerald Bonley, the new practitioner from the city, seduced by a lucrative practice sharply exaggerated by Dr. Stein, was hardly the type of doctor expected to set up his office in the small community of Wymans Creek.

He carried himself proud. His hard muscles strengthened by daily bouts with the recreational facilities of the big city. An outdoor man, tanned and sharp-eyed, fascinated by the lures of natural vege- tation, fresh air, and clean water.

The suits Dr. Bonley wore were expertly tailored, and he donned highly polished, high-priced oxfords. His dress alone placed Dr. Stein's appearance as unkempt and his approach uncouth.

There was a marked difference in the education of the two medical men. Yet each had the same title, General Practitioner. The prancing team of Babe and Bess was outmoded by the new shiny automobile the new doctor drove daringly over dusty country roads.

The new office was also modern and newly decorated. So great was the attraction of the new doctor that from the first day, the office was overcrowded with calls of various complaints. Though Dr. Stein was encouraged to see some of his old patients, he was stunned to learn that people he had not seen in years suddenly made an appear- ance in Dr. Bonley's sterilized abode.

The new doctor set his office hours from nine o'clock in the morning until five o'clock in the afternoon. In between those hours, Dr. Stein was often referred to in consultation. The new standards Dr. Bonley practiced could hardly compare with those of Dr. Stein, who had seen very few of his patients in the small cluttered quarters that served him as a kitchen and office. The new doctor made house calls only when the patient was too ill to make a personal visit to the office. If the patient were severely ill, he was transported some nine miles to Clarmourne's new hospital. This alone caused Dr. Stein great concern—the time it took to haul the patient to the hospital could cause serious harm. Of course, the hospital did have the equip- ment and trained personnel to speed up the healing process.

Early morning hours were often spent with Dr. Bonley in sur- gery or visiting bed-ridden patients in the hospital.

It was not unusual for the office hours to be delayed until mid-afternoon if the doctor was held up at the hospital.

Modern medicine, the old doctor concluded, often placed the patient's life in jeopardy. He had performed an appendectomy beneath the pale light of a kerosene lamp. Many a baby was delivered in a cluttered bedroom while the father and other children waited in the parlor. And he had sawed a man's legs off on a library sewing table.

Dr. Stein had bartered a slab of beef, a few chickens, or a good bottle of wine. Sometimes, cash would be handed him on the street. If it was a good year, people were generous. In bad years, he shared the suffering. It had been a satisfying profession for him—it had been just an existence for Julie.

The new office was equipped with modern gadgets that Dr. Stein had only read about in the Journal or had seen on an occasional visit to Clarmourne. Miracles were happening in the medical world.

There was much respect for the new medicine, but there was also a fear. The day would come when he would not have a patient. A certain lack of dedication was noted among the new breed.

They closed their offices right in the middle of the week. In Bonley's case, he closed every Thursday afternoon; on those days, he motored to the city to indulge in tennis bouts or play golf with some other medical cronies. The office was also closed Saturday afternoons and Sunday. All day Sunday.

It was as if the new men thought the patients could have a choice on just when they would become ill or when the baby would arrive, and they'd know better than to break a leg or arm on a Sunday.

Never had he put the sign Doctor Is Out unless he was on call or was incapacitated by exhaustion and resorted to the only thing he knew could give him sufficient rest for his mind and soul. Only in later years was he tempted by the devil, as he chose to put it. He trembled, thanking God that he had never lost a patient due to his weakness.

"God takes care of his own," he voiced. "He knows I try to abide by His law. Sometimes, I get sidetracked, but he knows what goes into the making of a good doctor. It isn't always what's on the outside that shapes a man into being what he is. It's how he thinks in the inside. Take Bonley—he's smart and looks like a Greek god, but he's cold as ice, using all those highfalutin words and running fancy new machines. And he drives that new automobile like he's crazy.

"A good doctor is born, not made. He's got a feeling for the suffering of other folk. It doesn't make one bit of difference who that person is. It takes a lot more than giving pills and shots in the arm. Some new operations can't keep a man alive. It's that extra pull from God, and it takes a man willing to give his whole soul until he's working in teamwork with the whole universe.

Things change, I know that—nothing stays the same. From day to day, there are changes. Old ways aren't always the best way—you've got to keep looking ahead, expecting things to get better. Once you stop and look back, you see you've already been there, so there's no place to go.

"Things change, and I've got to change with them. And my conscience will give me one big fight if I don't bring Dr. Bonley to the big house to see Lister and Wilkins. I know what he'll think, but it will burn like a fire inside of me when he doesn't say the things he thinks.

"Oh Lord, there are the miracles of birth and the mystery of death.

I can't figure either one out. I hang on to a bit of string, and every once in a while, I give it a yank and the whole wide world falls in on me.

"Next week, I'll bring him to Wymans Creek, maybe even take him over to meet the Old Indian Woman."

Chapter 1

· ·

DOCTOR'S DISAGREE

It was not the next week nor was it the next month. Spring had blended into summer; summer collided with fall.

It was late September before the automobile carrying the new doctor and Dr. Stein bumped over the Wymans Creek Bridge, scattering mud against the dropping branches of the willow and dig- ging ruts deep into the dirt road.

Chickens scattered, and the horses whinnied at the strange con-traption. Wilkins wheeled his chair closer to the porch railing for a closer look, and Rachel left Lister's bedside to survey the commotion.

It was a grim occasion for Dr. Stein who had longed to bring the new doctor on merely a social visit. Time had fled into the daily business of living. The call now was urgent. Lister Wyman was dying. It was Rex Paul, lean and tall with narrow hips and a shock of blond hair that startled the old doctor who had envisioned it to be auburn like Rachel's, who raced excitedly to climb on the running board of the car and run his fingers over the shiny metal. One look at the stranger with Dr. Stein sent the boy scurrying into the house to tell his mother that the doctor had a man with him; a sleek man in a city suit who looked just like the man selling the farm magazine last week. The man was driving a new automobile. Rachel hushed Rex Paul and stepped out onto the porch, shading her eyes from the glare.

Dr. Stein stepped from the car, holding the small of his back. "Hard as the devil on the back" was the only comment he made until he spied Wilkins. "Git back in the house, trying to catch your death?"

Wilkins wheeled the chair back into the parlor.

"Brought Dr. Bonley," he said to Rachel in a business-like man- ner. "I want him to take a look at Lister."

Rachel flushed. "She's in a coma since last night." Dr. Stein rushed past her to the library.

The big heavy brass bed had been moved from the upstairs bed- room to the library. A fire was burning brightly in the fireplace. Lister Wyman lay upon the bed, gaunt and unseeing, her head resting on a high pillow. Dr. Stein paused, then sat beside her on the bed, reach- ing for her hand. He felt for the pulse beat and shook his head.

Dr. Bonley handed him a stethoscope.

"There's not much life there," he said, handing the stethoscope back to the young doctor.

"This woman should have been in the hospital," Dr. Bonley said.

"Wouldn't have done any good. They'd just raised havoc with her, carting her all over the place."

Dr. Bonley looked at the old man with disgust.

"That may be true. But it's up to us to see that as long as there is life, the patient has every available chance. This was a case for the hospital. They have the facilities, and it would have been easier on the family."

"Bonley," Dr. Stein exhorted without the preceding title. "These are country folk. Some can't afford the luxury of the hospital. Some are plain against them. Lister is one of them. Her husband died in the hospital. He died full of stink and bedsores. She had her belly full then."

The new doctor was breathing hard.

"Like I said," the old doctor continued, "these people are ranch- ers and loggers. Most of the time, they just get by. You stick them in a hospital and try to get blood out of a turnip, you're up against it. That's why they keep a doctor in town."

"Just the same," Dr. Bonley said sharply, "she should have been in the hospital." He bent over the stilled woman, lifted an eyelid, and peered into her eye with an ophthalmoscope.

"What have you been giving her for pain?" he asked. "Morphine—I stopped by yesterday when I went down the creek to check on the old woman. Are you saying she's in a coma from a drug?"

"She's a goner, and I don't think it's natural."

"She's dying and it's as natural as living," Dr. Stein said, mop- ping at the perspiration now beaded on his forehead.

"Has she ever shown any toxic reactions?"

"No, when I left her yesterday, I knew it was just a matter of time."

"Get some coffee," Dr. Stein said quietly to the young doctor. "I'd like to be alone with Lister for a minute or two. I'd like to be with her when she goes. She was my friend for over thirty years."

Dr. Bonley put his instruments back into his case and walked from the room.

Rachel was seated by the kitchen table, her elbows resting on the linen tablecloth. She rose when Gerald Bonley came.

"She's going to die, isn't she?" she asked.

The young doctor sighed. "There's not much hope," he said, lowering his eyes.

"She's been sick for a long time, she's suffered so much," Rachel said, tears starting to well in her eyes. "Would you like some coffee?"

"Please," he said.

"I'm sorry I didn't offer you a chair," Rachel said, embarrassed. "I haven't had much sleep."

"That's all right," he said, sitting down.

She poured a cup of coffee and placed it before him. He took a drink of the coffee, then sat the cup down.

"She would have had a better chance in the hospital," he said. "She didn't want to go to the hospital," Rachel said. "She said that all along. Uncle Rex died in a hospital."

"That's what Dr. Stein said. Did Dr. Stein leave any medication for your Aunt?"

"No, he didn't leave any. He gave her a shot yesterday." Rachel swallowed and rested her hands on the back of a chair.

"Has she had anything since then? Medicine? Pills?"

Rachel looked frightened. "I gave her some of the Indian wom- an's medicine. Aunt Lister asked for it."

"What kind of medicine?"

"I don't know—homemade from some herbs or something." "Do you have any of it left?"

"No, it was only a spoonful. I gave all of it to Aunt Lister." "Rachel, that is your name isn't it?"

"Yes," she said.

"Are you sure you don't know what kind of medicine you gave your Aunt?"

"No, it was made from roots or leaves. Little Black Bear makes all kinds of medicine. She's Indian—real old. Lister told me to go and get it for her. The grandmother wasn't home, so Lalanne, that's her daughter, gave it to me."

"Did you know that it may have been a very powerful drug?" "No," she said, tears forming in her eyes again. "It was to make her rest more comfortably. She was in pain. The shot wore off right away."

"Did you tell Dr. Stein about the medicine?"

"No, Dr. Stein was out. Aunt Lister often used the Indian's medicine."

"Do you realize that this could be very serious?" he asked as if talking to a child. "That medicine could make your Aunt die."

"Dr. Stein said she would go anytime. He said he couldn't give her anything to help her."

"But Little Black Bear's medicine could?"

"Aunt Lister asked me to get the medicine, I did. I didn't make her die," Rachel sobbed.

He looked at Rachel, the little girl, not the woman.

All in one family, he thought. A child-woman and her gangly son, a dying woman and a legless man he had not seen yet nor did he wish to see him.

Dr. Stein closed the door to the library and put another log on the fire. For the first time, he saw the delicate chin lines, wrinkled now with age. Her hair was thin and almost white in contrast to her cyanotic complexion. How many times he had looked into that face and never saw beauty. *She was a handsome woman,* he thought.

"How's my girl?" he asked, knowing she could not hear him.

Her chest seemed to rise and fall before his eyes. But he knew it was his mind playing tricks on him again. He was just getting too old to practice. Sometimes, his eyes saw things he wanted to see. He thought of the modern hospital with the giant machines and white groomed attendants.

"You wouldn't have liked it there, Lister."

He took the pillow from under her head, fluffing it delicately, then put it back, holding her for a moment.

"Know, Lister, we've seen good times too. You're a real woman, not soft like Julie."

Julie again, even in the death of a friend like Lister, he would think of her. *I could have asked Lister to marry me. We could have had a good life together, but then, I'm a one-woman man. Julie spoiled it for me with all the rest.*

I could joke with Lister, and I was at home with her. She didn't expect nothing out of me that I wasn't up to.

"Lister," he said out loud. "That new doctor thinks I did this to you—swear to God, I didn't. Not to you. Sometimes I wished I could give you something instead of just watching you suffer, but when God makes up his mind about death, there's just no way out. I was a coward. I stayed away, so I wouldn't have to see you die in pain, but you're not gone yet. There's a thin thread that's making you hang on. It would be easier if you'd cut it."

Lister gasped. He raised her head higher to make her last breath easier. "I can almost hear the angel's singing. Take His hand, Lister, there will never be any more pain."

Tears started to fall, and he let them run down his face. "Dying's not easy, Lister, but you're a real trooper."

There was a small towel on the table, and he dabbed at his eyes with it. Lister had drawn her last breath, and he searched again for vital signs, but all functioning of life had stopped. He stood by her bedside for a few moments, trying to make his memory bring back the image of her when she lived.

He felt in his pocket for some loose change, then placed two copper cents heavily over her eyelids.

As he looked out the window, the sun clouded over. He pulled down the shade and gently covered Lister's face with the sheet. Then he picked up his hat and closed the door between him and the dead woman.

Rachel was waiting by the library door. Dr. Stein touched her arm, leading her away from the library.

"She went easy," he said.

"She's dead." Rachel sobbed. "She's dead, and Dr. Bonley says I made her die."

"That's nonsense, she died as natural as the day she was born," he said, comforting her.

"I gave her the medicine the Indian woman made, and it killed her."

"It wasn't any medicine. She would have died regardless. I knew she was dying months ago—so did she."

"Wilkins and Rex Paul Bonley will blame me, I know it! Doctor says I made her die."

The doctor glanced around quickly. "Where in the world is he?" The new doctor was leaning against the porch railing.

"She died a few minutes ago," Dr. Stein said. "There was no sense you are riling Rachel with that nonsense. She's high strung and nervous enough without you making her feel guilty for Lister's dying. You could have used some common sense."

"I'm sorry. I spoke quickly in there and out of order. There are still the facts, and we have to face them squarely," he said.

"The facts, Bonley, as I see them, are we have a dead woman in there, and we'd better get an undertaker. That woman died of cancer, and as far as I'm concerned, it's a blessing she went."

He was shaking and felt nervously for his pipe, filling the bowl with tobacco kept in a little bag, which he was having difficulties drawing closed. He lit the pipe, then puffed on it till the tobacco ignited.

"You know, Doctor," he said looking intently into Gerald Bonley's eyes. "I knew we'd see things a lot different. There is always a wall between the young and old. You think I'm old and obsolete. I think you're young and arrogant—it maybe we'll never see eye to eye."

"Dr. Stein," the younger doctor said sternly. "I don't think the thing we have to confront now is whether we'll see eye to eye. I think it's a lot more serious than that!"

Dr. Stein took another deep puff on his pipe. "I don't think I get what you're hinting at."

"That woman is dead. She is dead because of a dangerous drug.

Lucky for you, it was that girl that administered it." "Girl? Rachel?" he asked shocked.

"She said she gave the old woman some medicine made by some Indian."

"So? The Old Indian woman's harmless. Sure, she makes her own medicine. Tonics and cough medicine. Good stuff, too."

"Doctor, you are well aware that some pretty powerful medicine and drugs come from plants. Rachel said she makes it from roots and herbs. We had better look into it."

"Dr. Bonley, you're looking for trouble." "I think we've found it."

"If you're thinking about turning something like this in—better think again. These country folks aren't going to stand for you taking them for a fast city ride."

"There will be an autopsy, an inquest, heaven knows what!" Dr. Bonley said.

Dr. Stein chewed on his pipe stem. "There won't be! She died of natural causes and I'll swear to that!"

"Dr. Stein, in medical school—"

"Medical school! Rot medical school. Something like this stinks to high heaven. Don't go dragging anything like this up. It's the innocent that will suffer. God only knows that this family has had all the burdens it can handle. Forget it!"

"You seem to forget that I took over your practice, Doctor. On that death certificate, I have to put down the cause of death. In this case, it was the administration of a harmful drug that caused asphyxiation."

"You're jumping the gun, Doctor, the autopsy hasn't been done yet. Maybe they're teaching you something in medical school that I didn't learn."

"That may be true, Dr. Stein. You have your reasons for practic- ing the way you do. I intend to do one better—I plan on living up to my oath. Falsifying a death certificate is not valid in my profession." "It's my profession too," the old doctor shouted, his face becoming red with anger, then he quieted his voice, pleading. "I'm begging you, for my sake, to think it over. Think of Rachel and the boy. And Wilkins, that man doesn't have legs, and if you do, you might as well cut out his heart too."

Rachel stood and watched as the two doctors drove away. Billows of dust clouds were hanging over the horizon. So dark! As dark as the house is now.

"Rex Paul," she called, needing someone to reach out to, some- one to weep with and comfort her in her grief. Rex Paul did not answer her. She found Wilkins in the library; he had wheeled his chair beside Lister. Slumped and drunk, he was weeping while he grasped an empty bottle. Rachel closed the door behind her and ran sobbing out across the mud-spattered bridge, beneath the dirty branches of the willow tree. She kept running until she reached her childhood sanctuary, where she had often sat when she was a little girl, sitting and watching the Old Mother and Lalanne.

Chapter 10

. . . .

LITTLE BLACK BEAR —
GOOD MEDICINE

At dusk, Rachel spotted Little Black Bear, knee deep in the large leafed foliage that skirted the meadow. Digging at the roots that lie beneath the black soil, she extracted them gently, then knocked away the loose dirt before she dropped them into a crude basket. She lingered, waiting until she saw Rachel leave the knoll.

There is much sadness in the Wyman house, she thought, *but the spirit of Lister Wyman is not sad—it flies free without the sickness. My medicine is good medicine. Without pain, she finds peace.*

Slowly, to the far side of a cloud, the moon dipped.

"It is time to go," she said silently. "There will be no more dig- ging tonight. The light is gone."

When she reached the cabin, she entered but spoke no word to Lalanne, her daughter, nor did she glance at the young girl that lay asleep on the mat before the fire. She lit the lantern, then walked back toward the spring. Reaching the creek, she dipped the roots quickly into the water and shook the water from them before slicing them neatly and arranging them on a rack to dry. Her work finished, she walked stiffly back to the cabin. Before she went in, she lifted the glass chimney from the lantern and blew the flame out, then hung the lantern back on the hook.

Without removing her shawl, she raised the lid from the cook- ing pot that sat black and smutty on the big iron stove. She carried the pot with her to the table.

"Eat, Mama, it is good," the younger woman said.

The old woman's nostrils quivered as she dipped the spoon into the kettle, smacking loudly as she tasted it. She made a wry face. "There is no taste. You cook like a white woman."

"Mama," Lalanne said, "the older you get, the more critical you are. I learned to cook. I learned from books. I am a good cook."

"Good cook?" she said, reaching for a jar of crushed leaves, dropping a few pinches into the kettle, stirring the seasoning briskly. "Now, it is good," she said, bending over the kettle, inhaling the aroma. She ate a few spoonfuls from the kettle, then pushed the ket- tle to the back. She said, "Tomorrow it will be better."

Wearily, she took the shawl from around her shoulders, placing it roughly across her bed. Then she sank deeply into the feather mat- tress. Her eyes resting on Lalanne's child that lay asleep on the mat.

"The little one is weak. It is more white than Indian," she said to Lalanne.

"I am part white also, Mama, do not forget that." "I do not forget.

Your father, he was a good man." "I remember, Mama. He was a strong man."

"The little one's father is not good. He breaks his word. He will not marry you."

"I know that, Mama. But I will wait. When spring comes, he will be back."

"I will wait. You will wait. He will not be back. Tauna is nine years. How many times does he come? One time, maybe two times a year."

"He cannot come more Mama, I told you that! He has another woman, other children. They do not know of Tauna. His woman does not know of me."

"Someday, the little one will ask questions, she will want to live their way."

"Not for a long, long time." Lalanne knelt beside Tauna, touching her lovingly on the cheek. "I will keep her with me for a long time yet. I do not wish for her the way I wish for myself. I only want that when spring comes, I will see him again. For maybe one night, I will have him, and then, I won't think that he has another woman. Then I am the only one."

Tauna stirred in her sleep and Lalanne started to hum.

"We will see when spring comes," the old woman said, drawing the shawl over her shoulders.

Lalanne rose to blow the lamp out, then went to bed on the mat beside her child.

"Mama," she said after a long stretch of silence. "Lister is dead. I gave the medicine to Rachel."

The old woman grunted. "I know she'd die. My medicine is good medicine…she was in great pain, the medicine is strong, given only to bring a shadow over death."

"Mama, you should not have made that medicine."

"My word I give to Lister—when her time comes, there would be no more pain."

"Mama, even doctors can't do that! It is not the way they do things. Mama, you could get into trouble."

"Always you fret about my ways. The white doctors, they would like knowledge of the Indian. It has not been given them."

"Mama, your medicine is of old times. New times are here. It is better made in big factories, everything is clean. They do not need the medicine of the Indian."

"Maybe so. But my medicine is good medicine. See my fingers?" she said, holding her hands up in the darkness. "They were bent with pain. White man's medicine did nothing. I am old, they say. Yes, I am old, but I can walk without stick. I can weave. I can shoot yet the eye from a crow. Dr. Stein, he knows I have good medicine."

"I won't argue with you, Mama, you wouldn't listen to me anyway." There was another deep silence, then Lalanne asked wistfully, "Was that medicine really that strong?"

"Lister knows no pain now."

"I wish I hadn't given it to Rachel. There are laws!"

"Laws!" the old woman spat. "Laws, white man's laws. Traps to catch the Indian like coyote. Laws not right. Your father, he tells me that is so."

"Mama," Lalanne whispered. "How long were you and Papa together?"

Lalanne heard the quick, terse sigh of her mother.

"Hush, go to sleep, you take away my sleep. All night you talk with empty words."

"Did you love Papa? Like I love Tauna's father."

There was no answer to Lalanne's question, just the noisy threshing of the heavy body against the loose bed springs.

"Is something wrong? Are you in pain, Mama?"

"Pain? Yes, I am in pain, not of the limbs, but of the heart. Tomorrow, before the sun is up, I go back to the reservation. You are not Indian. The little one is not Indian, I am Indian."

Tears strained out onto Lalanne's hot cheeks. No, she was not Indian. She was a half breed, accepted not by the white man nor the Indian. Her tears would spill all night, and she would utter no word—never could she beg her mother not to go. But all the days ahead of her, she would be looking back, looking back and remem- bering the woman who had given her life and the disgust she felt for herself because she could not hold her close and plead with her to stay.

Lalanne ran her calloused hands over her bared arms. *Like leather, like the rough leather of my moccasins. There is a part of me I both love and hate. The blood of the Indian flowing through my veins, running over into my child, scarring her like an infectious disease.*

She snuggled close to Tauna, whimpering soundless far into the night.

The next morning, her mother was already out of the hut when Lalanne awakened. She lay and watched the sun creep in warm through the window. Like a cat, she stretched out long in the bed with an emptiness inside of her she had never felt before. A part of her life was cut out, and like a festered sore, she knew the time in healing would be long. Months and years of agony and remorse. Her mother's leaving would be deeply carved into her memories, haunt- ing her in the loneliness and stillness of each night.

So engrossed in her own sadness, she was unaware of Tauna looking at her strangely. Even the little one has changed. If only she could reach out and draw Tauna to her, lavishing the love she had never felt from her own mother, on her own love child. But some- thing kept holding her back from doing the things she longed to do. The years of rejection had been too long. Even a smile showing tenderness could not form on her lips.

"Get up, Mom," Tauna urged, scrambling onto the mat with a small dog that scampered over Lalanne.

"Get the mutt out and comb your hair," Lalanne cursed at the dog. This, too, was something she did not wish to do.

"Are we going into town?" Tauna seemed to welcome the harsh tones of her mother's voice. Always before, it was the old woman who told her what to do and scolded her. The old woman was gone, she heard them talking in bed. School would be different now. The kids would not yell at her anymore.

They would not call her the Indian's kid anymore. She would be just like the other kids. Mama was just like the other mothers—only her hair was darker and her skin browner, but that was from working in the fields. The sun had done that!

Maybe they would move away now. Maybe even as far as Clarmourne. She hated the smell of the sheep and goats.

The chickens stink! The shack stinks! All the kids in school stink! Mama looked sad again, and Tauna grappled with the dog and raced it outside. The big outside, where the sky was blue and the big white clouds hung loose in it. The sun was getting hot, and it sat up in the sky just like a big yellow mushroom.

Sometimes, the sun shone on the dew hanging on the grass, like diamonds. She put her hand under the blades of grass, feeling the cold, clean drops against her skin.

There was a depression in the ground, deep enough to hold water. Enough water that she could see her reflection in it. She stared at herself.

Her eyes looked back at her and they were gray. "Am I pretty?" she asked her mother one time. "Yes, you are pretty," her mother said.

"Tauna," Lalanne called, bringing her back from childish day-dreams. "Are you washed and ready? We're going to stop by the Wymans."

"I don't want to. I hate Rex Paul." "Why, I thought you liked him." "I don't! I hate all boys."

"Someday, you'll like boys—more than like. Maybe not now, but soon."

"No, I won't! I'll hate boys forever and ever. They make fun of my hair and they call me names."

"Boys tease. Just wait, soon you'll be making boys want you."

Mama says funny things, Tauna thought. She pulled the comb hard through her hair, her eyes smarting with tears.

She looked into the mirror. Even with the crack down the mid- dle, she was pretty.

"I'm pretty, Mama," she said, gazing at herself. Lalanne smiled. "Yes, you are pretty."

"Mama, why aren't my eyes brown like yours and Grandma's?"

"Your father has gray eyes."

Tauna ran through the door and fell face down in the grass beneath the oak tree. She was looking into a mirror again. A shim- mering, shaky mirror and then the sun hid behind a cloud. Tears fell into the puddle and the reflection was gone. But she felt torn in two—just like the time she had looked into the mirror and saw her face in two parts.

Chapter 11

DEFIANCE

The old Grandmother crept noiselessly through dense under-brush. Overhead, a buzzard soared, circling several times then flew down to a tree uprooted in the pathway, waiting and watching his intended victim.

The old woman took a stick and ran toward it. Flitting from its perch, the huge bird circled again and flew down to a higher branch—still watching her.

It was not fear for her own safety that prompted her defiance of the surveyer but the welfare of the old horse. Slowed by a limp when an unseen gopher hole made a trap for the animal, guided only by its instincts and led by an old woman. Little Black Bear followed the brush-covered path made with impressions left in her mind from the time earlier, when a young white man had led her to their new home. It was four moons from the reservation.

Through gullies and ruts left by men who had once logged with oxen and mules. Yonder a high cliff, blackberry vines tangling down the bank. The large fir now lacked bark, and many of its branches lay crumbled at its roots. A broken rail fence…she remembered the fence. The moon lay white in the late afternoon sky.

The horse's leg was swelling, and the horse was in pain. With wet leaves, she made a poultice, tying it to the foreleg with a length of sinew from her vest. As she worked, she chewed on a piece of venison jerky. The horse stumbled to the side as she sharply struck it on the flank with the flat of her hand. Sheltered from the wind now, she gathered dried firewood and piled it into a depression, banking it with stones. She would rest.

The bird was still sitting there at dusk. Turning her back to the vulture, she spat into the fire. "White man! Buzzards!" Her head nodding, she dozed. In her dreams, she saw Frederick, young and handsome, speaking to her father about her. Many horses he would trade just for her. Frederick took her to their new home. It was warm. It had a square iron box to cook on and a soft bed of feathers to sleep on. She heard the squalling of a newborn. There was the paleness of the white man in the child. Frederick called the girl Lalanne.

Fields of grain weaving in the wind, green in the springtime, amber in the autumn. How many of her children buried beneath those fields? Sons, dead when they were born. Another girl, dead of white man's sickness. Frederick gone. All gone, all gone by white man's curse.

Lalanne lived. Lalanne went to school with white man's chil- dren. When yet a girl, she had a child—that too by white man. And now, white man come to take old Little Black Bear, lock her in cage for making red man's medicine.

Only for a friend would she give her medicine. No, she had no friends. Shame they put on her child. Dishonor they put on the half-breed.

Darkness now. Darker by far than the nights she could remem- ber with the pale light of the oil lantern. The moon could show no light through black clouds. Coyotes circled around her and the old bird sat waiting to pick the meat from her bones.

"Why you not go south with the other buzzards?" she called. "You will eat, you will be so fat you fly crooked. Why you put the shadow of death on me?"

Thoughts ran berserk and wild, and she could not hold the fragments together. Cold biting wind stung through her blanket. She was shivering, and her teeth rattled. The cold was cutting off the blood to her head. High in the mountain and snow is coming.

Coyotes yipped. A lone wolf sent a curdling howl through the night. She started to laugh, and her laughter echoed. Louder and louder she laughed—at the sly bird waiting and the moon who could give no warmth. Then she was weeping for Lalanne who could show no tears for her leaving. While she was weeping, the echo of her laughter teased her—for she wept for her grandchild, whose eyes had told her she would be happy when she was gone.

In the morning, the horse had lost the poultice and was heaving and rolling on its side. From her saddle pack, she drew her rifle and put a bullet into the chamber. She aimed and squeezed the trigger. Neither fear nor remorse showed on her face. The horse would suffer no more. Putting another bullet into the chamber, she cocked it and shot again. This time, she shot at the vulture. She missed. What did it matter?

The reservation only four, five moons, she had lost count. An old woman, a dead horse, and did she not know she would never reach it.

Lalanne would think she was with her brothers again.

What brothers? They, too, long-time dead. Buried beneath plowed ground of white man. The white man stole the land. Where could the Indian bury their dead now?

The snow fell harder, covering the horse's body only a few hours dead. The old woman watched the fire as the log burned out. Black, it curled into smoke instead of warmth. Sleep, old woman… dream dreams of long ago. Frederick…green grass…black pony… Lalanne… Tauna—far more white than Indian. How long before the Indian be no more?

Colder and stronger the wind blew, blanketing the sleeping woman with the drifting snow. The lone buzzard left his perch, fly- ing to a higher branch, as hungry and crouching coyotes drew closer to the sleeping woman. The gray coals of the dying fire smoldered, surrendering to the drifting snow. One by one, the pack of coyotes, satisfied and content, moved back to the hills. Black feathers glisten- ing in the morning sun, the buzzard flew to the ground.

Chapter 12

THE TRIAL

The time span between the inquest of Lister Wyman's death and the hearing, naming Rachel Wyman as defendant was regrettable and unforgiveable. Wymans Creek, small town as it was, combined with the few thousand citizens of Clarmourne, the county seat, had little experience in handling an actual case involving highly technical legalities. Small courts in which horse thieves and cattle rustlers made headlines.

In twenty years, only two other cases were tried in court. One was a returning war hero, who had gone berserk firing wild shots in the neighborhood, mainly to put a little excitement back into his life after his worshippers suddenly forgot him. The other case: a sweet, charming old lady was questioned when three husbands disappeared in mystical fashion.

The veteran was captured and sent to a mental institution where he was released after spending six months sorting out little blocks. The little old lady confessed to living her life in trial marriages. If the union was not satisfactory, the men just went their own way. No official records of any marriages were found, and all the men were accounted for well and able. The case was dropped.

The case of Rachel Lansing Wyman caused a furor of divided opinions. Some claimed it was an injustice bringing such a limp hassle into the courts, using the taxpayer's money haphazardly. Others proclaimed it was the duty of the community because a human life had been escorted into death speedier than God's plan. Lawyers were not in agreement. If Rachel hated her Aunt enough to hasten her departure, it was murder. But if she loved her Aunt and wanted to help her out of her misery, it was mercy killing—not unheard of among medical men.

Complicating matters for the impending hearing, the Sheriff went to subpoena the Old Indian woman and Lalanne as witnesses.

The shack was empty, vacated mysteriously, no one knew when or where they had gone.

Rachel suffered loneliness before the arrest; it was torturous now. An illegitimate child living with an Aunt that had been a mother to her since she was five—even going as far as sending her to San Francisco to study art. Townspeople renewed the gossip of Rachel's return from San Francisco, the hasty marriage to Wilkins, and the short-term pregnancy. No one seemed to overlook the fact that in the Wyman home, Rachel and her son were the only ones to escape the physical agonies—almost as if she had plotted Wilkins horrible acci- dent and Lister's terminal disease. And if you really noticed, wasn't she always dolled up, like she just stepped down from a band box? Did she help Lister with the yard work or Wilkins with the chores?

Wasn't she always up in her room playing the piano or strolling out in the fields catching the eye of John Erickson's hired hands?

And wasn't it true that she received letters and a large portrait from some painter in San Francisco? Wasn't she always hanging on Wilkins even when he was married to Mary? Wild one like her mother.

If the neighbors and townspeople were cruel, the press was even more devious. Lister Wymans's small obituary notice appeared on page three, making headlines in just a few days.

The newsboys had a picnic digging for a good story, using their talents well enough to get every red-blooded citizen of the commu- nity up in arms.

Rachel needed sympathy, and she got it in a big dose from Dr. Stein. He refused to believe that such an incident could have taken such a turn. If Rachel was guilty of wrongdoing, surely, he was just as responsible.

Dr. Bonley was mystified that his sense of duty could have grown into such a monstrous dilemma. Regretting his hasty actions, he made ventures to make it up to the Wymans by working Thursday afternoons. Rehabilitating Wilkins, encouraging him to work with his hands, enthusiastic when he became an expert in leather tooling. Rachel viewed the situation in a mixed confusion, her world changing very little. Early morning hours were spent feeding and carrying for Lister's chickens. Trotting back and forth between the ranch and the County Agent, accepting and treasuring his advice. Afternoon hours were spent in her room, the door often locked. Her piano playing ceased and canvases flourished and were just as quickly destroyed.

Wilkins wished to show his sympathy, but Lister had been like a mother to him and doubts about Rachel grew. Cut off from a hus- band-wife relationship so long, now it was as if he were trying to contact a spirit from another world.

Rex Paul also seemed to have an insight into his mother's fears, but those were magnified by horrors of his own. His mother may have to go to jail—worse yet, die in the gas chamber or electric chair.

Handpicking a jury for the possible jury trial from the small list of taxpayers posed as much of a problem as the arrest itself. Old Ben had founded the town and Lister had married his son Rex some thirty years earlier. Very few had not heard nor known of the Wymans personally. It was Rachel who was the outsider, and tales of deceit swept from house to house as swiftly as a smallpox epidemic.

The few citizens not acquainted with the Wymans or attorneys in question were prejudiced by the local news coverage, accumu- lating vast reading audience in less time than one usually scans the headlines. Anyone hinting of libel or standing on the grounds of innocent until proven guilty were in danger of tar and feathers and being railroaded out of town. Wymans Creek was ripe for scandal. Free press, free country, and put the town on the map.

A jury was selected. Seven men and five women. To the attorney Dr. Stein had helped Rachel acquire with the total of his life savings as retainer, the jury was a favorable one. Especially, if he could initiate pity for the accused.

Harris Dewitt, Rachel's attorney, was likeable. Not chosen for his success as a small-town lawyer, but because Dr. Stein was acquainted with a client who in turn had instilled a faith for Dewitt's honesty and integrity, and he charged reasonable fees. In a day of shysters, this was indeed a favorable transaction.

Lloyd Hobbs, the prosecuting attorney, was reputed to be the stronger of the two lawyers, having had experience in city courts. Lloyd Hobbs was also suave, sporting a clipped mustache, over what the doctor proclaimed was a whiskey lip. Not that there were any logical reasons for the survey; it was just that the old doctor made quick appraisals. "I'm usually 99 percent right" were his exact words.

Plus, the fact that Hobbs had close-set eyes, meaning of course that he was shifty. Another of Dr. Stein's instant surmises.

Dewitt, on the other hand, dressed conservatively, was clean shaven, and looked intelligent behind big horn-rimmed glasses.

The Honorable Judge Jenkins, presiding, was born and bred in the community. Justice was his creed, vice, and in-bred heritage. Descending from generations of hard-fisted, tight-lipped lawmen. Of this breed, Judge Jenkins would be the last unless one of his four daughters broke the barrier of an establishment dominated by men. Until the Judge donned the cloak of justice, he could be taken for any businessman off the street of any small-town nesting in the valley. He had a thin beak-like nose, eyes that set deep, bald head, and pouched abdomen. But one only saw his eyes. Eyes that were black, seeming to have the ability of peering through objects. Of this man, Dr. Stein could make no judgment.

Judge Jenkins was admired as a man, and Dr. Stein regarded him as a friend, forfeiting many a checker game to him.

Now, he felt uneasy under the Judge's gaze—as if his life were rolling carpetlike before him, exposing all his iniquities.

The first day of the trial was windy and blustery, much as any early March day may be anticipated. A noisy courtroom generating a fierce-like heat—that of viewers being confined in galoshes and winter wools but mainly of excitement in an otherwise humdrum existence.

The groundwork had been lain for the trial. The stage set with the bailiff, lean and hog like, swearing in the coroner as the first witness of the people. The courtroom which had seen only assorted misdemeanors was now the center of a giant court procedure. People versus Rachel Lansing Wyman.

Rachel sat demure and innocent looking next to her attorney. She wore her hair down, and save for a slight powdering, she wore no other makeup. As advised by Dewitt, she wore a simple costume of brown wool with long sleeves and stark-white peter-pan collar, a simple hat, gloves, and patent shoes. Very much like a busy house-wife out on the town for a shopping spree.

The idea of Harris Dewitt was not to antagonize the women on the jury by representing Rachel as a beautiful temptress, but rather the ordinary housewife who could not possibly have a wicked thought in her head.

Wilkins was also in the courtroom. Dr. Bonley had made significant headway with the transformation. New artificial limbs fit securely in a new blue serge suit. Wilkins had not learned to use his new legs yet, but for the use of the wheelchair, no one would guess he was disabled. The relationship to Rachel did not register in his face; instead, he sat taking in the court scene as calmly as if he were watching a screen in a movie house.

Lloyd Hobbs, the prosecuting attorney, questioned the coroner.

Harris Dewitt declined cross-examinations. Other witnesses were called for the people. The defense withheld his cross-examinations, retaining the right to question later.

Whispers sped across the room when the first witness was called for the defense. Judge Jenkins hastily cracked the gavel.

Rachel's eyes met those of Dr. Stein's, for a moment smiling in appreciation to one who had been so loyal.

"Raise your right hand, swear to tell the truth the whole truth so help you, God."

The doctor was sworn in so swiftly, he was hardly aware of it. "State your name and be seated."

"Dr. Theadore Joseph Stein," the old doctor said, sitting down hard in the chair.

Dewitt loomed over him. "Dr. Stein, tell the court how long you have been acquainted with the defense."

The doctor cleared his throat and felt in his pocket for the out- line of his pipe. "Well, let me see. I was the Wymans' family physi- cian when Rachel's mother brought her to Lister. She was four or five then."

"How many years ago was that?"

"Don't recall exactly, maybe thirty years more or less. Can't say for sure—might tell my own age as well."

The audience snickered. The judge banged the gavel.

The questioning continued, and the doctor could not remem- ber how he had answered. Dewitt paced in front of him, sometimes glancing at a round pocket watch he had taken from his pocket. The chain had an odd-looking fob on it. Dr. Stein's eyes focused on the fob. and his mind strayed.

"Can you tell me, precisely, Dr. Stein, the type of relationship existing between the deceased and Rachel Wyman?"

"Like mother and daughter," the doctor answered quickly. "Rachel thought a lot of Lister. I'd say it was mutual. Like mother and daughter," he repeated.

"Would you say, Doctor, that Rachel was happy living with her Aunt?"

"Far as I know she was. Some kids aren't satisfied with their lot.

I think Rachel was. Lister treated her fair and square. Now, I'm not saying that Lister wasn't strict—"

"Do you recall, Doctor, Rachel ever harboring any ill-will toward her Aunt?"

"Naw, they just hit it off. Rachel wasn't one to sass, and like I said, Lister treated her fair and square."

Dewitt looked at his watch again, this time keeping his fingers wrapped around the chain as he put the watch back in his pocket. "Would you say that Rachel was unduly depressed over the illness of her Aunt?"

"Sure, she was depressed. It was a big load for her. She had a boy to care for and a man without legs. The old woman was dying of cancer. Of course, she was depressed. Who wouldn't be under those circumstances?"

"I'll do the questioning, Doctor." Dewitt seemed agitated with his witness. "What you are stipulating is that the defendant acted normal and natural regarding the conditions that occurred in the household?"

"Yes," the doctor said, convinced of the truth of his state- ment. "Tell the court in your own words, exactly what happened on September 21. Starting from the time you entered the Wyman home?"

"When? What was that date?" "September 21."

"September 21?" The date seemed to escape any special signifi- cance. "Oh, now I remember. That was the day Lister died."

"How did it happen that Dr. Bonley was also in the Wyman home on that particular day?"

"I object! Counselor is leading the witness." Hobbs raised quickly to his feet.

"Just tell the court what happened on September 21," the judge said without taking his eyes from Dr. Stein.

Dr. Stein shifted his position and glanced toward Rachel. He forgot what he was going to say. "Well," he fumbled, "everyone knows I'm past the age of being a good reliable doctor. So about a year ago—maybe more or could be less, I went to Clarmourne and talked to Dr. Bonley about taking over my practice."

"Dr. Stein," Dewitt said impatiently, "the court is only con- cerned with the facts pertaining to the day of Lister Wyman's death." "Yes," he said, shaking his head. "Now, on that particular day,

Dr. Bonley and I went to take a look at Lister. He had already seen most of my patients. Planned on seeing Wilkins too."

"Go on," he was prompted by Dewitt.

"I guess it was Rachel—no, it was her boy that came out to the automobile to meet us. Wilkins was outside, but I scooted him back into the house. No sense his getting pneumonia on top of his other burdens." He was stalling.

"All that gibberish is not relevant, Your Honor," Hobbs objected. "Your Honor, my witness is getting to the facts."

"See to it that he does," the Judge chimed. "Dr. Stein," Dewitt urged, "can we go on?"

"Well, the first thing Rachel says is that Lister was in a coma. Now, I wasn't shocked. I was expecting it. I looked in on Lister the day before, had to stop by and see the old Indian woman too. It was just a matter of time."

"What was the mental attitude of Rachel on that particular day?"

The doctor closed his eyes a moment and scratched at his chin. "That's a hard one to answer. You got to know Rachel. She can hurt like the dickens inside, but it doesn't often show on the outside. Like cooked mush inside. Sorta like Lister."

Dewitt was perspiring and rubbed a handkerchief across his forehead. "Was Lister Wyman in a coma?"

"She was dying."

"How did you base those observations, Doctor?"

Dr. Stein thought for a moment, then quickly replied, "My eyes, my ears."

"Was Dr. Bonley in the room at that initial examination?"

"Yes."

"In your examination, did you observe anything indicating an unnatural death?"

"She died a natural death," Dr. Stein said, weary from the constant hammering.

Questioning continued. The doctor tried to recall actual phras- ing of what had happened on that day. Memories of Lister dying haunted him, and he kept seeing her in his mind. A recess was called, and he stumbled from the chair.

Wandering alone down the hallway, mental agonies were con- fusing him. He visualized Rachel as Julie, and he couldn't remember if he had put Cat out. His mouth felt so dry, and he stopped to drink from the fountain. He still felt an awful thirst.

If only there was something to ease the palpitation and the pain circling in his chest like a steel ball. He put a nitroglycerin tablet under his tongue and staggered back to the courtroom.

"Lord," he muttered. "Tell me what to say. Words don't come easy to me. I just bungle my way through, and I'm hurting Rachel." Looking up, he saw Hobbs watching him from the doorway. The prosecution had seen him talking to himself. Well, he didn't care about that. "I'd never make one of them lawyers. Words slide from their mouths. I'm tongue tied, and my head is fuzzy."

The recess was over, and he was sitting back in the hard-backed chair again.

"The witness has been sworn in," someone said.

There was an exchange of lawyers, and Hobbs leered over him. Dr. Stein swallowed. Hobbs's shaving lotion nauseated him, and there was a bitter bile taste in his mouth.

"Dr. Steinberg," Hobbs said efficaciously. "Dr. Steinberg."

The witness gasped for breath. "Stein," he said, clearing his throat. "The name is legal. I dropped the Berg when I was in medical school."

A cruel glint showed in the eyes of Hobbs. Stepping back from his witness, he exposed the full view of Dr. Stein to the audience. He had hit his mark well. The witness was thrown off balance.

Harris Dewitt's jaw clenched, anticipating a secret alliance between his chief witness and that of the prosecution. He stood up facing the bench, his face red with anger. "Your Honor, the prosecu- tor is badgering the witness."

Judge Jenkins looked bewildered. "The witness has stated that his legal name is Stein. In this court, he will be referred to as Dr. Stein. Continue with the examination."

"Dr. Stein, we have heard your testimony in regard to the untimely death of Lister Wyman. Can you say in all certainty that Lister Wyman's death was not caused by the powerful drug made by some Medicine woman and administered to Lister Wyman by the defendant?"

The doctor's hand shook, and he reached toward his face, dab- bing at the perspiration with his shirt sleeve. "I can say with all cer- tainty that Lister Wyman did not die of any medicine, drug, or com- bination of drugs."

"Doctor, think about that question. Folk medicine, a poten- tially lethal drug given in a fatal dose to a person already critically ill. As a Doctor of Medicine, you are well aware that taking care of a very ill person over a long period can and does produce hostility and aggravations in the one burdened with such responsibility."

"No, as a doctor, I'm not aware of that! Sickness is my profes- sion—caring for the sick, that is. Rachel cared for Lister as well as any trained nurse, and she cared for her with love and compassion." "You stated earlier, Doctor, that Rachel Wyman had no ill will toward her Aunt. Isn't that what you said?"

"I said that. To my knowledge, there was never any sort of bad feelings between them."

"How old did you say Rachel was when her mother brought her to live with her Aunt?"

"I don't remember exactly—four or five, I think."

"Isn't it true, Doctor, that Rachel's mother left her with her Aunt, merely a baby. Does that seem natural for a mother?"

"Rachel's mother was a professional musician. She traveled with a road show. I'd say the mother was concerned for the welfare of her child."

"I object!" Dewitt shouted. "I see no relevancy to this case by continuing questions concerning the defendant's mother."

"Your Honor, I can prove relevancy."

The Judge was agitated. "Sustained. From now on, Prosecution will resist squandering time by asking questions that do not pertain to this case."

"Now, Dr. Stein, I'm going to refer to the drug again. The powerful deadly drug administered to Lister Wyman by the defendant. Could that drug have caused Lister Wyman's death?"

"And I'm going to answer again. No! Lister would have died regardless of any drug given her."

"We are talking about an immensely powerful, potent, deadly drug."

Dr. Stein's eyes lit up. "As far as I remember, there wasn't suf- ficient evidence of the mysterious drug—don't recall hearing in the Coroner's testimony that there was."

A startled attorney juggled for words. "You're very observant, Dr. Stein." He reached for a glass of water, took a swallow, and walked in closer to his witness. "In this modern day, a very ill woman died at home. Why wasn't your patient in the hospital?" Hobbs had changed his tactics.

The doctor became uneasy. There was another objection from Dewitt. "I object on the grounds that Dr. Stein is not on trial here. Whether or not Lister Wyman died in a hospital has no bearing on this case."

"Objection overruled."

The same question again. "Why wasn't Lister Wyman treated in a hospital?"

Dr. Stein coughed, then sipped from a glass of water someone handed him. "She had an adversity to hospitals. Old Rex died in one. She wouldn't be caught dead in one."

The court audience snickered. The Judge cracked the gavel again. "Order, there will be order in this courtroom."

Hobbs again. "Would it have prolonged Lister Wyman's life if she would have had specialized treatment?"

"Specialized treatment may have prolonged her life, it would have also prolonged her misery."

Hobbs placed his hands behind his back, pacing back and forth before the doctor. Now and then, he scraped his foot across the floor. It's as if he stepped in some manure, the doctor thought. The room was swimming, and someone handed the doctor another glass of water. Hobbs was still hammering at him, sometimes in a high- pitched voice, other times it seemed as if it was coming off a see-saw. Questions were being fired at him before he sifted them over in his mind. Accusations, seeping deep into his consciousness. Words slip- ping from his mouth and he couldn't control them.

"There are no further questions," Hobbs said, returning to his table. "The witness may step down."

Hobbs smirked, pleased at the response he felt he had drawn from the witness. A senile old man, an unethical medical doctor. A quack and a Jew.

No pleasure shown on the faces of the crowd. The prosecutor's tactics backfired. Tears were flooding many eyes. Rachel sobbed, not for her own pain, but for the castration of her friend.

When the doctor stepped to the floor, it seemed uneven and Dewitt escorted him out onto the courtroom yard. The trees had newborn leaves and a burst of green spread everywhere. But it was not new birth the old doctor was thinking of. It was winter. Leaves dry and crackled, scattered by the four winds. Hobbs had sapped the life from him and there would never be another spring.

It was a short walk down the middle of the road until he turned up the narrow pathway to his cottage. Cat nuzzled against his boots, and he picked the cat up and carried it into the house.

The fire was dead, and the house was cold. He took the milk from the window ledge and poured some of it into a dish. Without removing his coat, he fell on the unmade bed.

"Jew boy! You nailed Jesus to the cross. Sheeny Jew."

Holding his fingers tightly to his eyes, he tried to shut the sight out of his mind. Tears blurred his vision, and he felt the stab in his chest. He was a boy again.

"Joseph Steinberg," he heard his mother calling. "Who are you hiding from?"

Chapter 13

YOUNG JOSEPH STEINBERG

Young Joseph Steinberg stole softly through the back door of Steinberg's Kosher and Meats and passed the slabs of beef, lamb, and defeathered chickens and geese. The strong odor of vinegar and spices made his eyes sting, and he guided himself by touching the rows of barrels in the dimly lighted hallway.

"Joseph," his mother called to him. "That you sneaking in through the back door? Shame you can't come through the front door like the rest. Who you hiding from? Your Father? Me?"

Joseph stuck the book beneath his wool sweater. "I'm not hid- ing, Ma, it's a short cut."

"Short cut? What maybe one, maybe two steps?" "Yes, Ma."

"Joseph, don't forget now—don't bother your Father. All kinds of things worry him. If it ain't one thing, it's another."

He heard her mumble some more and quietly closed the door to the attic stair. As soon as he had shut the door, he flung down on his bed and opened his book. It had cost ten cents at the junk store. With big colored plates and big words, he had never heard before. *The Anatomy of the Human Body.* In amazement, he dwelt on the human body: muscles, bones, blood vessels, veins and arteries, and the organs.

There in the book big as life was what he was like under the skin. Just like the time he had taken his father's watch apart. He had pried open the back—wheels were grinding, and the watch kept on ticking. Before he had opened it, he would never have believed it took all those parts just to make it run. His father handled the livers and hearts of the animals he slaughtered for the butcher shop, but it never occurred to him that the human body was like that! And just like the watch, each part had certain functions. Each part could become faulty and stop working. With fascination, he studied the book.

Later, he heard his mother as she came to his room to blow out the lamp.

"Joseph," she said, "such a bookworm you are." Warm lips brushed his forehead, and he felt her gentle hands put another cover over him.

It was daylight before he stirred again. He wished he could shut out the sound of his father's voice bellowing at his mother. Though he could not see his father from the loft room, his father would be sitting at the kitchen table, still in his underwear and shouting orders to his mother. Such a loud mouth from such a small man, Joseph thought, smiling because he now stood a head and a half taller than his father and outweighed him by at least forty pounds.

His mother was scurrying back and forth between the table and the cook stove, yelling back at his father.

"OK, as soon as you quit your hollering, I'll call him," she said. His father's voice, "What are you raising that kid for?

"He's getting schooling, studying out of books all night." "Lazy bum! Reads books all night, sleeps all day. Now, when I need help. Mama, I say again, what are you raising him for?"

"Let me tell you big man. For a butcher? No! For a shopkeeper? No! Let me tell you, I'm raising him to be somebody. Maybe a big shot… like a doctor or lawyer. Maybe—"

"Maybe, maybe money, it grows on trees. You think school comes cheap? A doctor or lawyer?" His voice softened. "Better he works in the store and learn something."

"Joseph is smart!" she said proudly. "Here in America, you say this yourself. My son can be a doctor. My son can be president! A butcher, no!"

Joseph started down the stairway, waiting at the foot of the stairs until he heard his father's voice from the front of the store. His mother was scrambling eggs, and he stood by her side, watching her. "Come sit down and eat, then, like a good son, you will help your father in the store."

Joseph wanted to protest, but something in her voice bade him not to.

"Your father, he needs your help today. He had to let that Hobbs man go, smelling like a whiskey barrel he came to work today. A man with a family too, seven or is it eight little ones he has. Ach—such an unhappy day it is."

When Joseph finished breakfast, he put on a white shirt and one of his father's canvas aprons. He wanted to tell Ma he had heard what his father said. Calling him a bum, but what would it add to this day?

"Ma," he said. "I put my application in for medical school."

Tears formed in his mother's eyes as she caressed him. "See, I told your father you were a smart son."

"Ma," Joseph said, teasing her, "you said this yourself. Your son is not going to be a butcher!"

The same night, Joseph lay on his bed studying the book.

His father's loud snores echoed through the thin-walled build- ing. Dogs barked and whined. Placing the book across his chest, he closed his eyes thinking about his future as a doctor. How pleased Ma would be, Pa too—after he got used to the idea.

Glass shattered, something crashed to the floor. Loud voices, shouting, cursing, weeping. His mother sobbing. Looking through the attic window, Joseph saw his neighbors gathered beneath the pale gas lantern. Children he went to school with, throwing things at his father, calling him names. Everyone was yelling and screaming.

Hurriedly, he slipped into his trousers and stumbled down the narrow stairs. Stepping on pickles and vegetables that were hurled in the hallway.

His father's face was cut, and blood streamed out onto his underwear top.

"Go to your mother," he was shouting. "This thing cannot be, not here in America."

Later, he found his father lying in a small heap at the front of the store. His hands clutched to his chest and his eyes staring. A heart attack, the doctor said, but Joseph knew his father died of a broken heart.

For the first time, he knew there was something different about his family. His name was different! He had a different religion! He was a Jew!

Tears stung his eyes, as he remembered standing on the train platform clutching the old worn suitcase his father had brought to America, the worn fringe on his mother's shawl fading until he could no longer see her.

It never occurred to him then, as he left home that last time to go to medical school, that someday he would change his name, drop part of his last name and use his middle name instead of his first. But Ma said it best.

"To be a doctor, of that I am proud. But shame it is to your father's birthright to deny your faith."

The many years to deny one's faith. Hobbs, the years to sud- denly loom again and reveal all that he had tried to hide. Hobbs, the son of the man my father fired so many years ago. The pain stabbed in his chest. He did not reach for the tablets.

A few days following the funeral of Dr. Stein, Harris Dewitt and Lloyd Hobbs met in the Judge's chambers.

With the old doctor gone, it was evident that Hobbs had made a brief and disastrous mistake. Dewitt made no effort to conceal his distaste of Hobbs's ethics.

"You really made an ass of yourself, Hobbs, ready to make a deal? Dr. Bonley's hostile, and there are a couple on the jury that aren't exactly gentile. Perhaps, if you didn't carry such a chip on your shoulder, you would have noticed that you stepped on a few toes. I'm going for an acquittal."

Hobbs nervously fingered his mustache. "I can still make a case.
I can take that woman and tie this whole thing up."

"Hold it! This town would chew you up in little pieces. They didn't give one hoot who the doctor was or what he was. He spent his whole life administering to them."

"You're trying to force the issue," Hobbs was saying when the Judge appeared.

The two mature lawyers acted sheepish, like small boys caught in the theft of penny candy.

Dewitt stated his objections quietly to Judge Jenkins. "Your Honor, the passing of Dr. Stein has placed this case in a different perspective. Wymans Creek has suffered a great loss. At this time, I feel the court has been subjected to unethical procedure by the Prosecution."

Judge Jenkins spoke in reprimand. "It is indeed a sad day when the courts in this land submit to bigotry and racism. Hobbs, you're a disgrace to the profession. You deliberately took it upon yourself to put Dr. Stein in bad grace. And for what? Because he was living a disguise? It was his problem, not yours."

"I realize that, Your Honor," Hobbs said submissively.

"As for Rachel Wyman, whoever brought this injustice into court should have his head examined. The Coroner's report was suf- ficient to have thrown it out. Sadly, I'm as responsible as anyone. Prepare for the Jury's dismissal. I could kick myself for not throwing it out the first day."

"Yes, Your Honor," both men spoke spontaneously.

"One more thing, Hobbs, any more shenanigans in the court- room will find you on the other side of the fence. And I'll be the one to make the charges myself," the Judge announced.

"The press? Can I release Rachel Wyman's acquittal?" Dewitt asked, adding a "Your Honor" after the question.

"Oh yes, the press. The free press. Free to accuse, condemn, and maim. Think about that. If you didn't get anything else from this farce. The press handled it disgracefully—for all the story was worth. Newsboys are always on their toes and don't you ever forget that!"

The Judge looked very sad as he watched the lawyers searching for various legal forms. "This has been a sad session," he said wearily. "I was dragged along with the tide. I lost a close friend. I saw a young woman lost and bewildered. A man sat mesmerized in a wheelchair. Oh, how I pitied him! Then I saw a young doctor, fresh out of medi- cal school, get sucked in the filth. And I saw a good lawyer, smug and smirking because he crucified another Jew. And I saw myself. After twenty years on the bench, I got a close look at myself. All the time, I knew there was something unsavory about it. But I went accord- ing to the book, sitting unmoved like I was a godhead, labeling its procedure."

The lawyers shook hands and left the room. The Judge sat for a few moments longer, then he reached for his top coat and hat, leav- ing his gloves lying where they had dropped.

Drafts of warm air hit him as he left the courtroom.

The sun was shining, and birds were noisily welcoming the spring weather. But as he climbed into his automobile, he had to dry his eyes before he could drive.

There are some things, he thought, *tears cannot wash away. The loss of a close friend and the scandal and mental anguish of Rachel Wyman.* "Wyman Case Thrown Out of Court" carried banner headlines in the *Clairmourne Tribune* and *Wyman Creek Chronicle.* Just as the arrest had caused an avalanche of letters to the editor, so did the news of Rachel's release. The whole reading population sensed that something happened in the courtroom reeking of shady deals. Many feeling that injustice had been done, blaming the Attorneys Harris Dewitt and Lloyd Hobbs. Honorable Judge Jenkins presiding did not escape without nasty criticisms.

Then, just as quickly as the sensationalism gripped the public's mind, it became lost as news from abroad stole the spotlight.

World peace was threatened. Hitler dove headlong into the expansion of Germany, fulfilling his plan in Mein Kampf, and the Japanese bombed Pearl Harbor!

Chapter 14

WAR YEARS

War years were trying for Rachel, with day upon day filled with anxieties. As if to ax the multitudes of Rachel's fears and apprehensions, a wire arrived from San Francisco with the news her mother was dead. She had often toyed with the idea of visiting San Francisco, but the few times she had mentioned it to Wilkins, he had put up an argument and she pushed the thought from her mind.

Her mother's passing left her helpless and with regrets. More out of fear of having to face death herself someday than that of los- ing someone she had never really known. Rachel shed few tears and stayed home.

Thoughts of Paul Nielson seldom haunted her, but she often saw a fading glimpse of him in Rex Paul. Wymans Creek young men were going off to war before they finished high school, and when Rex Paul announced at the dinner table that he had enlisted, Wilkins was furious.

"If I stayed home," Rex Paul said, "everyone would think I was 4-F."

"What in the World do you care what anyone would think?" Wilkins cursed.

"Did it ever occur to you Dad, I want to go."

"No one volunteers to have his brains shot out."

"Maybe, I'd rather. I'm fed up with all the guff I take around here."

"You don't understand," Wilkins shouted. "This place is all we've got. Beef prices are way high, Rachel's hens are actually laying, and I've got a few orders—"

"You think you'll get rich making saddles and horse gear? Dad, for cripes sake, figure out the time you spend on the hand tooling alone. You're lucky if you come out even."

Wilkins looked at Rex Paul with a hurt look in his eyes, then wheeled his chair out of the room.

"Rex Paul," Rachel said, looking up from her book. "Dr. Bonley has done a good job with your father, he feels useful again. Don't spoil it. Even if he doesn't make a cent, it's something he can look forward to. Anyway, he's got a couple orders from Clarmourne and a special order from a rodeo performer in Wyoming."

"Big deal!" Rex Paul said scornfully.

The arguments between Rex Paul and Wilkins continued the next morning, growing into loud shouts and curses.

"Once in my life I ask for a little cooperation and—" Wilkins was shouting.

"And once in my life, I'm not buying it."

"Go to hades! I can run this place by myself. Don't think I couldn't do it. Even with—"

Rachel brought a basket of eggs into the kitchen. "The hens are molting, only twenty eggs."

"Who gives a hoot about her?" Wilkins complained.

Rachel looked stunned, breaking a dozen eggs as she put them into the cooler. "What's the trouble with you two?

"It's your kid. He thinks the Army needs him more than we do.

If I wasn't in this chair, I'd show her a few tricks." "Like what?" Rex Paul challenged.

"Like putting this ground back into production." "Fat chance! How?"

"Selling the upper section, that's how."

"You're nuts. The only way this place will pay is to get beef up there."

"And who's going to take care of them?"

They both looked at Rachel, her sweater matted with scraps of straw from the chicken house.

"Sure," Wilkins said. "We could raise beef like Rachel raises her chickens. If we didn't raise our own feed, we'd fall flat on our faces," Wilkins said with a ray of hope in his voice.

"Oh sure, Rachel's a real rancher," Rex Paul smirked. "She's not afraid to get a little dirt under her fingernails like you young punks are."

"That is enough out of both of you," Rachel said, trying to avert the heat of another argument. "The roof on the chicken coop is leaking, and I think you'd better get out and fix it before it rains," she said, looking at Rex Paul.

"And," Wilkins said, "you'd better drive me to Clarmourne tomorrow. We might be able to pick up a few feeders at the auction." "You're the boss," Rex Paul said. They heard him whistling as he took the hammer and apron of roof tacks out the back door.

"We can't make him stay," Rachel said to Wilkins after Rex Paul left. "It wouldn't be fair to make him stay just because we need him. Anyway, he's already signed up."

"He could get a farm deferment. And he owes us."

"No, he doesn't owe us. He's no different than any of the other boys. He wants to try it on his own. We'll just have to manage alone."

"We can't do it."

"I could help outside, do the chores, if you'd help a little bit in the house."

"Over my dead body."

"Then we'd better forget the beef."

"I'll be snookered," Wilkins muttered and wheeled his chair to his room.

It was nearly eleven that night when Rachel stopped by Wilkins's room on her way to bed. She wanted to go to him, to be close and feel comfort from his nearness. He was asleep, and she paused only a moment, then went to her own room. All through the years, she had Rex Paul, but he was leaving. The house already felt empty, and she lay awake a long time wondering how she would cope with her loneliness when Rex Paul was gone.

And then, before a new roof was put on the chicken house or loafing sheds built, Rex Paul received his orders to report to Fort Lewis for induction.

Raising beef was not the easy task Rex Paul impressed it to be. Grain sacks were heavy and throwing out bales of hay and straw for bedding was tedious and strenuous for a man, let alone a petite woman like Rachel. Fences badly in need of repair were left stand- ing only because a weak wind had not blown their way. Tansy grew everywhere on the ranch, and the government was issuing bulletins warning of the danger of the weed to cattle. Rachel pulled the weeds out by hand and propped the fence posts here and there.

Ranching for Rachel meant getting up before the sun and weary enough for bed with the sunset, but household chores prompted her to stay up nearly half the night. She lost weight under the heavy burden, and when she appeared in a pair of Rex Paul's blue jeans, Wilkins chided her.

"I've got to wear something on my legs," she explained.

"I think I have the tansy whipped, now blackberry vines are growing all over the place. If I don't chop them out, who will?"

"For goodness sake, get some spray. Go to the feed store and rent a sprayer," Wilkins said, irritated with her dullness.

"The county agent said we should put alfalfa in the lower field. Two, maybe three crops a year. It'll build up the soil and maybe make some money on the leftover hay," Rachel said.

"I never thought it would be like this," Wilkins said sadly. "You are working your butt off and I am just rotting away."

"I couldn't do it alone," she said, her eyes meeting his. "Wilkins, we'll make it. A little at a time."

"Rachel," he said her name gently. "I hate to see you worn out all the time. Ranching is a man's job. You're a woman."

His words of tenderness pleased Rachel, and she wanted to say something nice to him. Tell him how much she needed him. But she couldn't say them.

It rained hard until late June, but the months of July and August were hot and dry. Bone dry. There was one light cutting of alfalfa, but it was a first-year crop and it had been a late wet spring, probably needed reseeding.

With the absence of the rain, the waterhole in the upper section dried up. Rachel hauled water in milk cans, but the small quantities did not satisfy the intense thirst of the cattle. She spent another day bracing the rotted posts by the barn, so she could drive them down to the water tank.

Wilkins wheeled his chair to the fence, watching as Rachel herded the half-crazed animals to water. Thin flanked, bulging rib-cages, bellies stained with mud, shoving and butting each other, forc-ing their way to water. Tears came to his eyes when he saw Rachel riding in behind them. Her hair was prematurely gray with dust, and her jacket was torn.

"I've got to get back," she called to him from the saddle. "One of the steers got out."

Before Wilkins had time to object, Rachel was loping back toward the rangeland.

The wind had arisen, and dust churned over the flatland. Wilkins watched her ride away until she was lost in the whirling dust. Rachel, in her haste, had forgotten that he needed help up the steps.

It started to thunder. Lightning flashed. Sharp, streaked bands of fire that seemed to strike the dirt. Clouds blackened and rolled. A thunderous burst spooked her horse and it reared. Fighting to bring the horse in control, she slid from her mount, talking to the horse, trying to calm it. Darkness glided in around her. Twigs snapped, and she thought she heard sheep bleating, but the sound was deadened by another clasp of thunder. Listening for the bawl of the steer, her senses seemed to dull, fear nagged her. She remembered Wilkins was outside and couldn't get back into the house alone.

She mounted the horse again, and the saddle started to slip, and she stepped down to the ground. It started to rain, sheets of water pouring from the sky as she fumbled with the cinch strap. Trying to lead her horse along the fence line, the blackberry vines were like a jungle and she couldn't walk through them. A thorn snagged her pants, and she heard the rip and felt cold air on her bare flesh. "Ouch!" she cried. Lightning zigzagged across the sky and she cringed.

If only someone would go to the house. But people seldom called now. Not since the trial and not since the war.

Many of the women worked the ranches while their men drove many miles to work in the defense plants, sometimes only coming home for the weekend.

All the young men were at war. Rex Paul was at war. Fighting a war for his country, and fighting a war within himself. She felt guilty. Rex Paul was now a man, yet she feared for the boy. Casualty lists were endless, pages of dead, wounded, or missing in action. In her mind, she counted the boys from Wymans Creek, only three were on the list, but what if one were Rex Paul?

Rex Paul wanted to go. What was wrong at home? He preferred dying to living. How he must hate her, blaming her for Aunt Lister's death. Maybe he even blamed her for Wilkins accident.

If I hadn't loved Paul. If I wouldn't have had Paul's baby. She shivered. *I wouldn't have Rex Paul.* A deafening thunderbolt ripped through the sky, shaking the ground under her. The horse stopped, refusing to move. Rachel jabbed her toes into the horse's ribs, then struck it sharply with a twig that for some reason she still held in her hand.

The horse stood in determined stance. Rachel cursed and begged, but the horse would not move forward or backward.

When Rachel looked up, she saw a dim light. For the few moments the horse refused to move, she regained her sense of direc- tion. The light was coming from Little Black Bear's shack.

Leading the horse down the grade easily, Rachel tied the reins to the oak tree, then rapped loudly on the door. Lalanne came to the door. A much older Lalanne with graying hair and drooping bosom. Rachel raised her hand and brushed her own damp hair back from her face.

"Rachel, you're soaked through. Is something wrong? Come in," she said, holding the door open.

"I was lost," Rachel said, her voice weak and shaky.

"I couldn't find the fence line. I've got to hurry. Can I borrow a flashlight, a lantern, anything? I left Wilkins outside when I went back to look for one of the steers."

"He'll find shelter, he's bound to," Lalanne said, reaching for the lantern.

"But what if he doesn't?" Rachel said.

Lalanne shook the lantern; it was almost empty. "I'll fill it," she said, pouring kerosene into the base. She struck a match and held it to the wick. "There it is. I'll have Tauna go with you."

The young woman that appeared from behind the curtain, now separating the sleeping quarters from the living room, was no longer the shy little girl Rachel remembered. Tauna was a woman now—a slender, lovely creature with glossy hair and large eyes.

"That is Tauna?" Rachel asked surprised.

"It's been a long time, hasn't it? I couldn't stay for your trial. Mama would have got into trouble. She was so old, it would have killed her," Lalanne said.

Rachel looked worn. "It's been a long time, sometimes I don't think it really happened."

"I wanted to help you," Lalanne said. "I really did!"

It had stopped raining, but there was a drizzle, cold and dampening. Darkness was black without the light of a moon. In the distance, dogs were barking, intermingling with the yipping coyotes. Neither Rachel nor Tauna spoke. Silent tears trickled down Rachel's cheeks. Wilkins was probably sick, and it was her fault. Such a long, hot summer, and they needed the rain. *But not today,* she wept, *we didn't need it today.*

The horse's hoofs made hollow echoes across Wyman Creek Bridge. A light shone in the summer house. Why hadn't she thought of that? There were no steps to the summer house.

Wilkins sat huddled in his chair, but a fire crackled in the wood stove.

"Where in the devil were you? I was worried sick," he said at the sight of Rachel.

She thought, *If he only knew how worried I was about him.* "I didn't find the steer. It started to pour, and I couldn't find the fence line. It stormed, and—"

"You were a fool to head up there after dark," he said quietly, noting Rachel had someone with her.

"Lalanne's home. Remember Tauna?" "You mean that's Lalanne's kid?" "She has grown up hasn't she?"

"Sure, as blazes has. Get me into the house, and both of you get into something dry. Rachel, you look like a drowned rat."

Later, Tauna stood before the painting of Rachel.

"That was painted when I was nineteen," Rachel said. "An artist in San Francisco."

"You were beautiful!" Tauna looked at Rachel strangely. "Your eyes look different. They look sad! But I guess you've been through a lot."

Rachel turned away. The girl's familiarity triggered a tinge of resentment in Rachel.

Tauna ran her fingers nimbly across the piano keys. Shivers climbed Rachel's spine. The keyboard hadn't been touched in so many years.

"I didn't know you played," Rachel said. "I had lessons in Phoenix," Tauna said.

"Will you play something for me—after we get into something dry."

"I really don't play well—would have been better, but we had to leave Phoenix."

"Didn't you want to come back to Wymans Creek?"

Tauna shook her head and tilted it haughtily. "Oh, I don't know. Anywhere is better than Wymans Creek."

"You can sleep here," Rachel said to Tauna, showing her Rex Paul's room.

"Don't you sleep downstairs with Wilkins?" Tauna asked. "No," Rachel said quickly, not looking at the young girl. "Because of the accident?"

"No, since before the accident." "That's sad."

Why, Rachel thought, *do I have to be so honest?* Stripped of her private haunts yet it was so nice to have someone to talk to. It had been such a long time since she had talked to anyone since Rex Paul. "You can sleep in, Tauna. I'll fix breakfast when I finish the chores."

"It must be hard being married to someone like him. You have to help him a lot, don't you?"

"Yes."

Tauna had a questioning look in her eyes. "I'll bet there are lots of boys coming home from the war like that."

"Oh, Lord, I hope not. I can't bear to think of things like that!" Rachel said quickly.

"When do you think Rex Paul will come home?" "I don't know. When the war is over, I suppose." "He was smart in school."

"He did very well in school," Rachel said proudly. "I was dumb!"

"I know you weren't dumb," Rachel said, feeling pity for the girl.

"Maybe not stupid dumb but dumb. Never got good grades, mainly Cs and Ds. Never got an F, though."

"Did you finish high school?"

"Nope. Mama wanted to come back to Wymans Creek, so I quit."

"Well, you can finish school now."

"No," Tauna said determined. "They'd remember I was the Indian woman's kid. It would be just like before."

Rachel looked at the clock. "It's late, better get some sleep."

She wanted to pull the covers over Tauna's chest like Aunt Lister used to do. Aunt Lister would put the quilt way up under her chin, then she would blow the lamp out and tiptoe out of the room as if she were already asleep. But Tauna was not a little girl.

"Remember what I said about sleeping in," Rachel said, closing the door.

Back downstairs in the kitchen, Rachel put on the tea kettle. When the water boiled, she made tea and sat by the table, sipping it slowly. Strong winds were blowing, and shrubbery scraped the siding of the house, making strange noises. She left part of the tea in her cup and went back to her room.

It was a long time before she fell asleep. How very much Tauna reminded her of when she was a young girl, she thought. Thoughts of Tauna were scrambled in a dream, riding the mare in the marshland. The horse disappeared, and it was Wilkins. She was holding him above murky water. He pulled at her, trying to drag her along with him, but she didn't sink. She kept floating on top of the water as if she were as light as a dried thistle seed.

The sun filtered through the curtains the next morning when Rachel awakened, making a zigzagging design on the wall. She had overslept! Hurriedly, she dressed and went to Rex Paul's room. Tauna was still sleeping.

Wilkins was sitting on the edge of his bed, trying to put on his shirt when Rachel came to his room.

"Let me help you," she said.

He drew away from her. "I can get it myself," he said, flushed and breathing heavily.

Rachel placed her hand on his forehead. "You're feverish, better stay in bed. I'll bring you some coffee."

"I feel like hades. Caught a blasted cold last night." "It was my fault," she said.

"I'll be OK," he said, struggling with his shirt.

He started coughing, and she helped him back into bed. She bent to kiss him. It was an impulse, and she wondered if it was guilt that made her experience such a feeling of warmth for him. Wilkins reached for her and drew her close to him. But the moment of ten- derness turned to torment.

"Get out of here! Out!" he said roughly. "Get out and stay out!" "I'll call Dr. Bonley."

"Like hades you will, just leave me alone."

She looked back at him as she left the room. Tears were stream- ing down his face. So many times, she had wanted to hold him and comfort him, but he would never let her get that close. Not ever.

Chapter 15

REX PAUL COMING HOME

Months crowded in on one another, melting years into bygone days that seemed never to have happened. Season followed season. Spring, Summer, Fall, and lonely months of Winter crept into another Spring

It was Spring of all seasons that Rachel looked forward to the most. Fuzzy, peeping chicks arrived in the mail. For days, Rachel kept busy disinfecting water jugs and changing the litter. A constant check was kept on the brooder's temperature. With the arrival of the chicks, other signs of Spring were imminent. Young heifers dropped their first calves, and the steers were moved to a new grazing pasture. But it was this Spring that made Rachel happier than any other. Rex Paul was coming home! The war had been over for several months, but only now did it seem true. A wire arrived saying Rex Paul would reach Wymans Creek on Tuesday afternoon.

The Army man stepping off the train was mature now with hardened eyes and a tight mouth. He had spent many months on foreign soil, weathered many battles, and lost some of his most prized men. Second Lieutenant Wyman was well trained as a soldier, an officer, and now back home, he was a stranger.

When Rachel went to the station to meet Rex Paul, she had a queasy feeling in her stomach. He had gone away a boy. Now, he was a man. She wondered what she would say to him.

What he would say to her.

As she walked through the station door, she saw Rex Paul sling his duffel bag down to the floor, pacing nervously. Watching as his eyes roved to a couple of young girls that were laughing and talking loudly. *How much he looks like Paul,* she thought.

He sat down on a bench for a moment, then walked to the window. Rachel touched his arm.

"Rex Paul," she said, not embracing him.

"Oh, hi, Mom," he said, dropping a cigarette to the floor, squashing it with his foot. "I was wondering if you'd meet me."

"Do you have all your things?" she asked, walking out to the parking lot.

Rex Paul picked up his baggage and followed her. "I'll drive," he said when they reached the truck. "Know when you wrote you bought a new pickup, didn't dawn on me that Dad couldn't drive it. Funny, how fouled up you get when you're away."

They drove through the town silently. *Rex Paul is home,* Rachel thought, *he's home, and I can't find anything to talk to him about. My own son and it feels as if he's someone I just met.*

Willow branches brushed the cab of the truck as they reached the other side of the bridge.

"Everything looks different. The creeks just a dribble."

"Yes, I remember when I came home from San Francisco. Nothing looked the same."

"Know something, Mom, I could have been home months ago. Could have come home when the war was over. Was in Italy, sorta fell apart afterward."

Rachel sighed. "You're home now. That kept me going, know- ing you'd be home again."

"Yeah! Me too, I talked with the Chaplain, when I was still in boot camp. Could have got out on a dependency discharge. Can you beat that?"

"I know," Rachel said.

"Seems nuts, doesn't it? I went through so much, and I could have been home."

"It was your decision. We didn't have the right to interfere." "When did you cut the vines from the back porch? Makes the house look smaller. Still needs a paint job."

"We've done a little at a time. Maybe we can get at the painting this summer. The chicken house still needs a new roof, tarred it, but it still leaks."

"Say, how's Dad taking it? You running things? He had to get his own way though, didn't he? Shouldn't have sold the upper sec- tion. I tried to tell him to hang on to it. Got cheated, too."

"Don't rub that into him. It just got too much for us."

"But you could have made it big. A couple hundred head or more if you'd irrigate."

Wilkins was making supper when they got home. He threw the potato peeler into the sink when he saw Rex Paul.

"You on KP, Dad?" Rex Paul said with a grin.

The two men looked at each other, then Rex Paul embraced Wilkins roughly.

"You're looking good, Dad."

"I'm glad you're home safe, son," Wilkins said, fumbling for words.

Rachel finished the supper while the men went into the living room. She felt crushed when she heard them talking and laughing.

Rex Paul's absence had drawn them closer; it had put a gulf between her and her son.

Tauna came through the door just as Rachel was finishing up with the dishes.

"Is Rex Paul home yet?" she said excitedly.

"He's in the living room with his father," Rachel said, following after the girl.

"Do you remember Tauna?" Rachel asked Rex Paul.

He looked at the girl, studying her. "I remember a skinny kid with long braids down her back," he said.

"I remember you, Rex Paul," Tauna said, her eyes flirting.

All that night, Rex Paul thought about Tauna. Laughing gray eyes mocking him.

The next morning, Rex Paul got up early, after spending a restless night. Coming home wasn't as he anticipated it to be. Not that he expected a hero's welcome, big bands, and such, he just thought his mother would have been happier than she was. He had thought about them all the while he was gone, hoping they'd be so glad to see him, they'd fall apart. His Dad looked so old and he had changed. It was hard picturing him, helping with housework, knowing how much it hurt his ego.

It was five-thirty. The sun wasn't up yet, and low fog hung like blue smoke in the meadow. His stomach was tied in knots, and he felt totally mixed up.

The pickup motor was cold, flooding a few times before it started. There was nowhere to go, so he drove up and down the back roads. Wymans Creek had grown, mailboxes with names he wasn't acquainted with. Some of the roads had new tar, and for stretches along the road, survey ribbons marked new construction. He parked in front of the John Erickson ranch. New barns and new loafing sheds. A white board fence made the ranch look prosperous, and he felt envious. Their ranch might have looked like that if he would have stayed out of the army.

Yellow and orange streaks stretched across the sky as the sun came out, and he drove along the creek road. The old Indian's shack looked more run down than ever. Tauna had changed though. God, what a few years does to a girl. He drove up to the knoll, where he could see the Wyman Ranch buildings to one side, and the shack on the other. How the ranch had deteriorated. Not that he blamed his mother, some things women just can't do. She expected him to stay home now. Wymans Creek didn't have a thing to offer. He was an Army man. He rehearsed it over and over in his mind, how he was going to break the news to his folks.

"I'm going back in, make the service my career," he wished he could say, but he knew it would not be that simple. Smoke was curl- ing from Little Black Bear's shack. The old shack always held a fasci- nation for him. Taboo, the old Indian woman was considered to be a witch doctor, and he was always afraid of her. Tauna strolled out into the yard. He grew tense. Watching her as he had once watched the Krauts. Waiting until they were close enough to fire upon. His heart pounded, and his fists clenched. The war was over. He was home, but there was still that panicky sensation in the pit of his stomach.

Fear, the kind that makes cold sweat break out all over you.

She was picking up scattered pieces of dry kindling, wearing a loose frothy-looking housecoat. When she walked out from the shade, he could see the slimness of her legs through the gown. Full breasts moved with her when she stooped to pick up the wood. A twig snapped, as she stepped on it.

The old Indian Woman was full blooded Indian, but Tauna's steps fell heavily, not the stealth of an Indian.

Rex Paul threw a stick in the air; it fell a few feet away from Tauna. A frightened gasp came from the girl. When she saw Rex Paul, she tossed her head back and held her hands to her hips.

"You scared me," she said.

"I didn't mean to," he called, then climbed down the grade till he stood beside her. "That's why I threw the stick—to let you know I was here."

"Well, it isn't funny."

He looked at her closely, baring her body through the flimsy material. "You've grown up."

"Isn't that what you expected?"

"I just can't get over it. I remember how I used to tease you when you were a little kid."

"I had to wear braids. All the boys in school pulled on them," she said, tossing her long hair to the side.

"Did it hurt?" he asked as if he felt her pain.

"Yes, it hurt! But it didn't hurt as much as when they called me names."

"I never!"

"No, maybe you didn't, but everyone else did."

"You were an awful pest though, tagging me all over."

"You were mean to me too," she said, pouting. "You told me to scram."

"I wouldn't say that now."

She took his hand, drawing him beside her on the grass. "I'm not the Indian woman's kid now, am I?"

"No," he said weakly, feeling her hand on his.

"Rex Paul," she said, flirting and taunting. "Do you think I'm pretty? As pretty as the girls you met when you were overseas?"

"Prettier," he said, drawing her to him and kissing her mouth. For several weeks, they met secretly in the morning.

One day, Tauna said to him brazenly, "Rex Paul, are you going to marry me?"

"I wouldn't make a very good husband," he said, pretending he wasn't shocked.

"Oh, yes, you would! You'd make a good husband, a good father also."

He pushed her from him, feeling a sense of panic. "I'd make a lousy husband."

But then, she was doing things that left him weak, wanting to spend a lifetime of holding her.

Later, she sat apart from him, mocking him with her eyes.

"It would mean living in Army dumps," he said hurriedly. "You can starve to death on Army pay, and I've seen cockroaches five inches long."

"I'm not afraid of bugs," she said wide-eyed. "No kidding, we used to live in an apartment above this cafe in Phoenix. There were bugs, even rats. I wouldn't be afraid of anything, not ever, if I were married to you." Nesting in his arms, she was silent for a while, then she said, "I'm glad the war is over. I was afraid you might never come back again. Know something? I've slept in your bed. Did your mother tell you that?"

It was almost noon before they started down the pathway to the shack.

"You will marry me," she said, clinging tightly to his hand. He did not reply.

"We will get married, and I'll be a lady like your mother. We'll have three—no, maybe two babies. A boy and a girl. The boy I will name Noble, and the girl—"

"Hey? Isn't it customary for the man to do the proposing?" "Yes, but not with you."

He hugged her tightly.

"Why not me? Am I different?"

"Rex Paul," she giggled. "You're afraid of love. I felt that in your arms. You've known lots of women, I felt that also."

"I've known lots of women," he said boastfully, but when he looked at her, his boasts stuck in his throat.

"I'm jealous," she said, tearing away from his hold, running ahead of him.

When he caught up with her, he felt like crushing the breath from her for tantalizing him. She drew away from him and placed her fingers across his lips.

"Noble," she said softly. "That's if it's a boy."

"You're counting your chickens before they're hatched." Ignoring his remark, she started to reminisce. "One time when Mama and me were in Phoenix, this man came to see Mama. His name was Noble. He looked just like an English nobleman or some- thing. He was so good looking, and he was nice to me too. Don't you think that Noble sounds rich? Like it belongs to someone special?"

Rex Paul started to walk away. Tauna called after him. "It is a nice name. Don't you like it, Rex Paul?"

Rachel was throwing bales of hay to the stock when Rex Paul reached home. He could tell she was angry.

"Where were you?" she demanded. "I needed the truck to haul hay to the steers."

"I was checking the fences," he said defiantly. "There's a lot of grass up there. It would save a lot of work if you'd get those fences fixed and move the young stock up there."

"John Erickson said he'd put in some new posts, soon as he gets his spring crop in," Rachel said.

"You might as well sell the bottom ground," he said, changing the subject. "It's wet nearly the whole year round. The Alder's just right for cutting. The mill should give you a good price."

"We were waiting until you got home. Get a chain saw and thin it a little at a time."

"You know! I'm not sticking around. I never said I was." "No, you never said you were. I just thought you'd want to."

"I'm not staying. Can't you and Dad get that through your heads?"

Words flew from his mouth so differently than he had rehearsed. Rachel started to corral the young calves back into their pen. She didn't say a word, but he did not miss the look of despair on her face.

Rachel went to her room early that night. When Rex Paul went up to say good night, she was at the piano playing "Since You Went Away," waiting until she had finished the song before speaking to her. "When did you start to play again? I haven't heard you play since I was a kid."

"A couple of years ago. Tauna used to practice—before I knew it, I was playing again."

"Nothing Tauna does surprises me." "She's very talented," Rachel said.

"I'm going to marry her before I go back in," he said, watching her face for reaction.

Rachel stopped playing and walked toward the window, draw- ing the window shades abruptly. "Do you think that's such a good idea? She's very young and immature."

"She's been around."

"Get to know one another better."

"For goodness sake! I've known her all my life."

"Sometimes, you think you know someone, but you don't know them at all."

"You're talking about Dad, I suppose."

"I'm not talking about anyone in particular. It's merely a fact." "Did you ever love Dad? You never even slept in the same bed." "There are some things I can't explain, not even to you."

"Like what? That's he's a drunk and a cripple."

"Please, Rex Paul, he'll hear you. He didn't want me," she said quietly. "Even before you were born, he didn't want me."

"That's a lie! It's because of his legs." "No," she whispered. "That isn't true."

She started weeping, and Rex Paul slammed the door and went downstairs to join Wilkins.

Her own son, she wept, making her feel as if she were not a complete woman. Defending Wilkins, wanting to tell Rex Paul the truth. What was the truth? Wilkins wasn't his father, he was not even a Wyman. If he knew the truth, he would only hate her more. How could she beg him to stay when he did not wish to stay? And how could she ask him not to marry Tauna? He would marry her out of defiance.

Oh Lord, she thought, *if I could only start my life over again.* To start over again or to die. The simplicity of dying. She envisioned Aunt Lister and Dr. Stein, without the protection of the coffin. Decomposing, worm-eaten, decaying flesh.

Life is so short, so short, and so many days of not living at all. Sometimes, it would be easier to die, but I'm afraid of dying. Afraid, because of Aunt Lister's hades. God, haven't I paid enough for my sins? She began to drowse. *But I'll have to pay. Pay for loving Paul and pay for not loving Wilkins.*

Chapter 16

WYMANS CREEK WAS GROWING

The next morning when Rachel awakened, Rex Paul and Wilkins were already out of the house. The coffee was made and set on a cold burner. She reheated it and poured a cup.

Without bothering to eat breakfast, she put on her sweater and went out to do the morning chores.

It was mid-afternoon when she cleaned the eggs and put them in the cooler. The house seemed so quiet without the men, and she opened the kitchen curtains looking out of the window for a glimpse of them.

So many things had changed with the years. Wilkins was no longer dependent on her. Rex Paul was home again, but he wasn't going to stay.

Across the fields, she could see how close the construction boom was to the ranch. Wymans Creek was growing, swallowing acres and acres of farm land. If they sold off the bottom land, only forty acres would be left. Forty acres out of all that land!

Electric wires drooped near the back door. Electricity had made things easier for her, a new washing machine and vacuum cleaner. She had only dreamed of things like that.

Now, a floodlight lighted up the whole yard at night, and the county agent suggested leaving the lights on in the chicken house all night. The chickens would eat more and lay more eggs. So many new things in such a short span. There was less work with water piped into the house and outbuildings, but she still went to bed at night exhausted.

It was dinner time when Wilkins and Rex Paul came into the house.

"Went to the depot to pick up some rawhide," Wilkins explained. "Got a couple new orders."

"You could have told me where you were going," she said, annoyed that they had crowded her out of their lives.

Rex Paul was washing up in the kitchen when Rachel approached him.

"When are you leaving?"

"The nineteenth," he said bluntly. "That's only two weeks away."

"I'm marrying Tauna next Friday. Nothing fancy, Justice of Peace."

"I wanted you to have a church wedding," she said, not wishing to sound apprehensive.

"We don't have that much time," he said, slinging the towel across the back of the chair.

"Does it have to be in such a hurry? Couldn't you—"

"Rachel, quit griping at him," Wilkins said crudely.

Putting the food hurriedly on the table, Rachel did not look at either of them as she sat down to join them.

"Honestly, I hate leaving you guys in a mess," Rex Paul said. "I just can't hack it—Wymans Creek's dead!"

"They're hiring at the hardwood mill," Rachel said. "No dice," Rex Paul said and left the table.

The next day, Tauna brought material and a pattern for her wedding dress, asking Rachel to help her sew it.

They were in the library when Tauna tried the first fitting. "I'm so excited!" Tauna said as Rachel adjusted the bodice. "I always knew that someday I'd marry Rex Paul."

"Is that what you really want?" Rachel asked, hating herself for asking such a personal question.

"It's what I want, more than anything else in the whole world," Tauna said, caressing the satiny material of her dress. "I'm so sure I love him—so very, very sure. He loves me too, more than anyone he ever knew."

"When I was seventeen," Rachel announced, "I didn't have the slightest idea what love and marriage was all about."

Tauna looked at Rachel. "Have you been happy? Married to Wilkins?"

The bluntness of the question stunned Rachel. "I've been happy," she said her voice quavering. "I suppose I could have been happier."

"But were you ever really and truly wildly in love?" "Yes," Rachel said.

"You know, I thought I was in love one time in Phoenix. There was this boy in school. He was Mexican. Mama didn't want me to go with him, so sometimes, I'd tell her I had to help the teacher after school. I'd meet him down by this vacant lot. Most of the time we just talked, but," she said wistfully, "it can hurt so much when love goes wrong."

"I know!"

"I was fifteen then. Mama said I wasn't even dry behind my ears. She wouldn't let me go out. She's too protective, like she wants to keep me home with her all my life."

Tauna took the dress off, laying it across the table.

"Do you think I'll make a pretty bride?" she asked, then without waiting for Rachel's answer, she said, "I wanted to stay in Phoenix, but Mama wouldn't let me stay there alone. She was afraid I'd get into trouble or something. I hated her then, but I'm really glad now. If I would have stayed, I might never have seen Rex Paul again. I'd just die if he was getting married to someone else."

"What did your Mother do in Phoenix?" Rachel asked.

"Oh, she was a housekeeper for this man. I had my own room, and there was a piano. That's where I learned to play."

"Didn't your mother like it there?"

"I don't know. Carl even wanted to marry her, but Mama said she couldn't marry someone she didn't love. That's why we moved. We moved to this apartment, right above a cafe. Mama worked in the kitchen, it was crummy. There was this man though, that came to see Mam sometimes. He was really nice. I wished Mama would have married him, but I guess he was already married. His name was Noble, ever hear of that name before?"

"No," Rachel said. "It is different."

"He and Mama talked a lot. I slept on the couch in the living room. I'd pretend to be sleeping, but I couldn't help hearing what they said. He wanted to stay with us while he was in town on busi- ness, but Mama said that would be living in sin. Do you know what he said then? He said I was conceived in sin."

Rachel glanced in pity at the girl.

"He said I was conceived in sin. Mama said I was born of love. When Mama said that, he said any baby born out of wedlock was born in sin. That sounds sad, doesn't it, to be born in sin?"

Rachel felt a familiar ache.

"When I was little," Tauna continued, "I didn't even know a baby had to have a father. I thought I just belonged to Mama. The kids in school used to call me names."

"Children can be cruel. They say things without even thinking. Sometimes, they don't even know what they mean."

"You didn't have a father either, did you? Oh, I know you had a father, but your mother wasn't married either. Mama said your mother gave you to Lister when you were just little. She used to tell me that, so I wouldn't feel so bad. She kept me, she said, because she loved me more than anything else in the whole world. Did you feel bad about your Mother, like it was your fault?"

"I used to feel awful when anyone hinted that my Mother was bad—that hurt the most."

"Want to hear something funny?" Tauna said, laughing. "Do you know the first time I knew babies had to have fathers. I can hardly believe I was that dumb! I used to have to herd the sheep up to the pasture past the old mill road. Well, I took the sheep up there one day, and the ram got caught in some barbed wire. He had big crooked horns and I was scared to try to get him loose. He was bleating and looked right at me like he was begging me to help him. I took the ewes down and was afraid to tell Mama he was still stuck in the wire.

"Mama asked me where the ram was. I said he was still eating and didn't follow me down. The next day, I took the rest of the sheep back up there and he was dead. Something had been eating on him. Every time Mama or Grandma asked me about him, I lied. A long time later, Mama got another ram, but when lambing time came, we didn't have any new lambs. Mama said that the old ram was probably too old, and the new one too young. I told Mama I lied about the ram. I always thought he was just like an old watch dog."

Rachel smiled. "Perhaps your Mother found it hard to discuss mating with you. Aunt Lister never talked to me about it either."

"Mama never told me anything—not even about my monthly. I was so scared I thought I was bleeding to death. I wish Mama was more like you. I can say anything to you. You don't act shocked or nothing."

"Your Mother has had a hard life, Tauna. She probably wasn't able to talk to her Mother either."

"I know, she's had it hard. But she never even listens I talk and talk—she's always busy. When I told her about Rex Paul, it went in one ear and right out of the other. Even when I told her I was going to marry him."

"Does your Mother object to you marrying Rex Paul?"

"It's nothing like that! She likes Rex Paul. I think she's even glad I'm getting married. You're glad we're getting married, aren't you?"

Rachel thought about the question before she answered.

"I think it would be better if you waited awhile, until you're eighteen and until Rex Paul makes up his mind what he wants to do."

"He wants to get married now." "I'm sure he does."

"But you don't want him to marry me, the Indian woman's kid?" "I didn't say that! I want a happy marriage for you both."

"I know I can make him happy. And I will sleep with him always, no matter what would happen to him."

"Tauna," Rachel said curtly. "My marriage to Wilkins hasn't been perfect. I've tried to be a good wife—perhaps, I've been noth- ing more."

"You're a lady, Rachel, you're smart and you can do lots of things. But I want to be a woman also."

"You are a woman, Tauna, and as a woman, you shouldn't be so quick to judge me nor my marriage with Wilkins."

The two women now looked with scorn at each other. Rex Paul came into the room, and Rachel quickly placed the dress on the hanger.

"We can finish tomorrow," she said to Tauna, who was staring at her as if she were another person.

Chapter 17

REX PAUL AND
TAUNA MARRIED

The summer following the wedding passed quickly. Communications with Rex Paul seemed to have snapped off for Rachel. Short notes arrived occasionally from Tauna, but personal letters from Rex Paul were few and distant. A brief curt note reached Rachel in November. He was stationed in Germany with the occupational forces, Tauna was to follow him in the Spring.

Thanksgiving and Christmas uneventfully dragged into New Year's Day, loneliness etching deeper for Rachel. A cold snap hit, freezing the water pipes in the kitchen. Rachel wrestled with a pipe wrench, weeping in dismay when she discovered she did not know how to do plumbing. Water covered the floor and flowed under the hallway carpet. She was on her knees trying to sop it up with towels when Wilkins banged on the door.

"Let me in, Grandma."

Sobbing and disarrayed, Rachel opened the door.

"What in the World? Don't you know enough to turn the water off?" He cursed, handing her an envelope with Tauna's limp scrawls on it.

"Why didn't they tell me?" Rachel sobbed. "Why didn't they tell me?"

"Get the handle they laid on that kid." Wilkins grinned.

"Della Rae," Rachel wept louder and couldn't stop.

For several days, Rachel knitted frantically on a yellow sweater set for her first grandchild, fussing that the baby would be half grown before she got it.

Several weeks later, a thank-you note came with a letter and snapshots of the baby. She and Della Rae were flying to join Rex Paul in Germany.

Less than a year later, another announcement arrived. "Major and Mrs. Rex Wyman are the proud parents of a baby boy. Noble Benjamin Wyman." Rachel shivered. Her grandson carried Old Ben's name without a trace of his blood, and the name sounded like it came from some Gothic novel.

Early the next morning, Rachel drove to Clarmourne to buy the baby a gift. She decided on a sterling silver cup with his name engraved on it.

Driving home, her thoughts seemed to be unrelated and flicked from San Francisco to Rex Paul, to Paul, then back to Wilkins.

Where have all those years gone? A grandmother and she couldn't even remember herself as a mother. It started to rain, and her thoughts kept time with the slapping windshield wipers. Rehearsing a letter to Rex Paul.

A new Junior High School is being built in the fill by the Old Indian woman's shack. John Erickson passed away, and a big grain company bought the ranch. They've already started on the grain ele- vators. Dr. Bonley has a new partner, they're talking about putting in a Medical Clinic. In Wymans Creek…think about that!

Your Dad got four new orders for custom saddles. The City Dads are sponsoring a Rodeo and Frontier celebration for the first part of June. The men are growing beards—should see your Dad's. She felt a bump. The pickup jerked to the side. She'd forgotten to have the tire checked. Wilkins warned her about it. She slipped in the mud, changing the tire, and her hair was lank and straight, and she had wrecked her shoes.

Tired and worn, she bypassed the kitchen when she got home. Wilkins was angry. It was stupid to drive all the way to Clarmourne for a present. She knew about the tire; he had told her, how many times? Too tired to argue, she ran the water into the tub.

Everything was changing. Wymans Creek was changing. Even the seasons seemed to change. Springs were earlier; nights when frogs could be heard croaking along the creek in mid-January.

Sometimes frost hit as late as June followed by summers that were hot and dry. Other times, mid-March saw the last chilly nip. Winters appeared milder, then a late snow fell deep and banked. On those days, Rachel shoveled a narrow path to the mail box, barn, and chicken house. Young heifers clustered close to the barn and the chickens quit laying.

Rachel was seldom seen in town in feminine dress, usually donning western cut jeans and sturdy shirts. She always wore a scarf over her hair. Some said it was to hide the gray. Women still snubbed her, viewing her as some kind of a threat. Though Rachel was hardly the lady the men remembered, they were polite, and their eyes still followed her.

Time was dimming the pains of the past, and days passed when the gossip mongers never mentioned her name.

If Rachel was lonely with Wilkins spending much of his time working in the leather shop, she treated her loneliness like a disease, curing it by hard physical labor. Townspeople were amazed at her physical stamina—here was a woman, cultured and talented, run- ning the Wyman Ranch as if she were born for the position.

Wilkins was regarded with equal awe. A man seriously handi-capped was succeeding in a business and rapidly becoming a popular candidate for the town's mayor.

If the marriage of Rachel and Wilkins was not an ideal union, a gap had been bridged by companionship and respect. Wilkins boast- ing about Rachel's artistic design on a saddle he was tooling and Rachel respecting his advice on ranch management.

Rachel started to paint again. She carried the easel and paint box to the knoll overlooking the Little Black Bear's shack, isolated like a mirage. On one side, the low-roofed Junior High School, meticulously landscaped ultra-modern with tinted glass. On the other side, the temporary rodeo grounds, cornered by great mounds of soil pushed to the side by the giant machinery.

Rows of aluminum-sided campers and chrome-decorated pick- ups caught the sun's rays, reflecting in the creek water like a lost ancient city, misshapen and distorted in the ripples. Debris floated on top of the water, then caught by a whirling pool, tails pinned into an uprooted tree that leaned into the water. Glass shattered! Empty beer bottles splintered against the rocks. The swimming hole where no one dared to swim anymore.

Shouts of excitement from the Rodeo echoed. An ambulance screamed. Rachel put her hands to her head trying to shut out the piercing sounds, wishing for the peace of bygone years when the knoll was her sanctuary. Birds singing, flowers blooming, the years when the only intruders were chattering chipmunks or a rabbit nibbling on clover. But even the sounds of the grain harvesters and the whine of the saw mills were sounds that could be heard no more.

Laboriously, she climbed farther up the hill, farther away from the sounds of progress and time. She was breathless when she set up her easel again.

A lone butterfly soared freely flirting with her arm as if search- ing for a resting place. As it took flight, a pheasant rooster startled her. Two gray squirrels chased back and forth until they spied her, then scrambled up and over an old cement foundation. The old mill. She had walked in a complete circle.

Directly below her sat the Old Indian woman's shack. Weather worn tarpaper siding, tattered and bulging where tacks had fallen out. Missing shingles on the roof patched with cutout tin cans like miniature mirrors tossed there haphazardly. The rail fencing dappled gray by many rains, bent and swaying as if in tune with the breeze. Hanging lopsided on broken rusted hinges the gate squeaked loudly, sending chills up her spine. Deterioration by the lack of man's pres- ence. She felt a closeness to Lalanne.

Shadowing the entrance, the oak tree looked grotesque. Rachel counted the panes in the windows—nearly all were mended with masking tape.

The sun basked lazily in the late afternoon sky, bathing the horizon in dusky pink-tinged film as it blended with the smoke from the mills and the dust from the rodeo grounds.

Leaves from a diseased tree ripped away in the breeze, floating rhythmically, then malfunctioning like a torn-winged butterfly, fluttering, dying, falling to the ground.

It was June, yet there was the feeling of Autumn—as if time had raced ahead of her, and at this moment, she had caught up with it.

More leaves, fragile and crisp fell around her. Rachel felt giddy and lightheaded, scarcely noting the beauty of the bronzed sunset. Then she saw Lalanne, her skin tanned like leather from the daily contact with the hot sun, herding the flock of sheep through the gate. But it was not Lalanne Rachel saw—it was the old Mother, quick and agile, holding a pose Rachel had only captured in memory. The Indian proud of a heritage loving her work and her land.

Rachel's brush seemed to whisk independently of conscious control—catching the colors of Autumn leaves and coral-striated sunset, the reds, yellow, oranges mixed with the greens and lavenders. Painting the foliage as nature intended, forgetting the disease that had made it wither and die.

When she had completed the picture, she rubbed her eyes as if awakened from a dream. Folding the easel and carefully protecting the canvas, fearful less it blur, yet stamped permanently in her mind's eye. A vision she had seen so long ago, completed stroke for stroke in colors she never believed she dare use. So dazzling that the beauty of it blinded her. Now she had preserved it. The talent still lived in her, more perfected than she ever dreamed possible.

She looked across the landscape. A passing era. The bottom land filled in by tons and tons of fill dirt, sides of mountains gnawed into and carried away. Steel monsters arousing dust clouds as far as the eye could see. More homes were being built—cracker box sitting on cracker box.

Lurking on the west side of Wymans Creek, the smoke stacks of the factories and the ugly wigwam burners of the saw mills. Thick, gray smoke billowing and destroying the natural beauty of the land. The ranches seemed to have been crushed out of existence.

Closing her eyes, she sought to momentarily bring back the views she wanted to paint the most. Grain fields that stretched for miles and miles. Green in the Springtime, amber in the Fall. Acres of cool valley nesting among the crests of the sloping hills, cattle grazing, horses prancing and lambing time, counting the black dots among the white.

The rise of the mountains, covered with trees reaching heights of glory, the cool clear brook, even the marshes with its skunk cab- bage and cattails.

She still felt weak and dizzy. Things might have been different if it weren't for Wilkins's accident. We could have farmed the land. Now Wymans Creek grew and gathered the land in tentacles, spread- ing and gnawing further into the farm land, gobbling up even the wastelands no one ever dreamed would be worth a fortune. Finally, Wymans Creek had no place to grow. The forty acres she was stand- ing on was like an oasis in the middle of a cement jungle.

Wilkins was nowhere in sight when she reached the house. She went directly to her room, holding her eyes to the top of the stairway. The distance seemed so great and she was so tired.

Carefully laying the canvas on the dresser, she fell down onto her bed. The chenille bedspread felt rough; caressing it, she remem- bered the satiny touch of her bed in San Francisco.

Above her bed, the portrait Paul painted of her appeared to live and Rachel smiled back, thinking, "I was young like that once. I was in love with the artist that painted that."

Paul's face came before her, and she fought to hold his memory. But it faded, and she felt empty again.

A car door slammed, and men were talking. Wilkins showing some cowboy his leather shop. *Wilkins needs me. We made a go of the ranch. Only forty acres left. We can live off that! And I can sell my paint- ings. All these years I dreamed I was a great painter. Something I really felt in my heart. Every joy, every pain I've lived through. I've painted the face of the old Indian woman, and I painted the land I've loved—that she loved.*

The young girl in the portrait swirled above her, and she lost focus as her vision dimmed. Green grass, cushiony and cool caressed her feet as she ran wild and free across the meadow. Soft winds kissed her cheeks as a brilliant stair way beckoned. Aunt Lister's voice kept repeating, repeating, "The song of the sparrow. I've heard the song of the sparrow. Are not five sparrows sold for two farthing and not one of them is forgotten before God! But even the very hairs on your head are all numbered. Fear not therefore, ye are of more value than many sparrows."[1]

"Rachel," someone called her name. Wilkins needed help up the stairs.

---

[1] King James version. Luke 12:6–7.

Acknowledgment

I would like to Thank my friend Albertine (Tena) Ellinwood for allowing me to use her Photography in this book and the books to come. She is a Professional Photographer that I had the pleasure to work with on an assignment at a Jewelry Store. The owner was a Client that my Sister Tami Patzer advertised for. Tena took the photos of the Jewelry, and I wrote down what they were. It was a wonderful experience seeing how a Professional Photographer worked. We became good friends and even

127

years later stay in contact. With her photography, I know that this book will be a beau- tiful addition to anyone's Library. If anyone would like to contact or see her Artwork, here is her contact information: http:// www. tenaphoto.com/ tenaellinwood@yahoo.com

About the Authors

Author - Margaret Wiese

Margene Wiese-Baier is truly her Mother's daughter. Growing up seeing her Mom's love for the written word. Her Mom is not only a Writer, but an Artist in her own right. Passing on the Legacy to write in her own Unique style.

Margaret taught her daughter Margene about Jesus from a young age, and seeing her love come alive in her wanting to share with the World what He did for them. Also, passing on what she was taught to her own children. Margaret always wanted to go on Mission trips, but due to Health issues and raising a family, did not fulfill that Dream, but Margene was able to go to Honduras and India to share what she had been taught not only by her Mom, but the Holy Spirit, leading her to the right people. In doing this, she felt that she was not only making her Father in Heaven happy but was bringing her Mom's dream to pass!

Co-Author -
Margene Wiese-Baier

Margene always had Dreams of her own to becoming an Author of a variety of books. In Publishing her own books and now getting her Mom's books Published, she is making those Dreams come true. Being able to co-author her Mom's books is a wonderful experience. Not that it has been easy. The enemy has fought her in this venture. Making her know how much more they need to be done.

As we go on our Journeys in life, we are going to see things in our own lives that are going to baffle us on how compassionate Our Father is toward us and to others, Forgiving us for our sins that others will see as unforgivable.

There are Messages in Margaret's Novels that have value that needs to be shared. As do all of her writing. Margene has been on a Journey to do the work for Abba Father. She has been Prophesied over that she would reach the Nations. Not knowing that through Social Media that she is truly doing this. She has turned many of things that she has written to share into Inspirations for her book *Angels in Flight* and her Children's books, *Kiwi and Kiki, Joy of the Jungle,* a story of a young girl going on a Mission trip to Africa. Also, her book about her cat Kobie.

One thing that she has learned through her Mom's books is that those without sin can cast the first stone. Thinking of the story in the Bible of the woman that was found in Adultery. Isn't it amaz- ing how no one could throw a stone at the Woman and Jesus was compassionate and told her to go and sin no more? Throughout the Bible, there are many stories of Immorality, but the Lord used them as lessons to help us be better people. David had a man killed so he could Marry his wife. Yet He was still called a man after God's own Heart. Solomon wrote the great Love story called Solomon's Song, yet he had many wives and concubines.

Through Margaret's and Margene's writing, their Prayer would be that it not only Honors Abba Father, Jesus, and the Holy Spirit, but it will bring a Wisdom to people that He has a plan for their lives, and that sometimes if Dreams are not fulfilled in their lives, that it is carried on being fulfilled by their Children.

May God Bless you and yours!

www.ingramcontent.com/pod-product-compliance
Lightning Source LLC
Chambersburg PA
CBHW051209120626
46547CB00013B/1270